UNDERSTANDING YOUR CROSS ROADS WITH GOD'S DIVINE VIEWPOINT

John R. Spiker

PublishAmerica
Baltimore

© 2012 by John R. Spiker.
All rights reserved. No part of this book may be reproduced, stored in a retrieval system or transmitted in any form or by any means without the prior written permission of the publishers, except by a reviewer who may quote brief passages in a review to be printed in a newspaper, magazine or journal.

First printing

PublishAmerica has allowed this work to remain exactly as the author intended, verbatim, without editorial input.

Softcover 9781462678730
PUBLISHED BY PUBLISHAMERICA, LLLP
www.publishamerica.com
Baltimore

Printed in the United States of America

COPYRIGHT INFORMATION

Scripture quotations marked (NLT) are taken from the Holy Bible, New Living Translation, copyright © 1996, 2004, 2007 by Tyndale House Foundation. Used by permission of Tyndale House Publishers, Inc., Carol Stream, Illinois 60188. All rights reserved.

Holy Bible, New Living Translation copyright © 1996, 2004, 2007 by Tyndale House Foundation. Used by permission of Tyndale House Publishers Inc., Carol Stream, Illinois 60188. All rights reserved. New Living, NLT, and the New Living Translation logo are registered trademarks of Tyndale House Publishers.

The text of the Holy Bible, New Living Translation, may be quoted in any form (written, visual, electronic, or audio) up to and inclusive of five hundred (500) verses without express written permission of the publisher, provided that the verses quoted do not account for more than 25 percent of the work in which they are quoted, and provided that a complete book of the Bible is not quoted.

COPYRIGHT INFORMATION

Scripture quotations marked "NKJV™" are taken from the New King James Version®. Copyright © 1982 by Thomas Nelson, Inc. Used by permission. All rights reserved.

The text of the New King James Version® (NKJV®) may be quoted or reprinted without prior written permission with the following qualifications:

Up to and including 1,000 verses may be quoted in printed form as long as the verses quoted amount to less than 50% of a complete book of the Bible and make up less than 50% of the total work in which they are quoted; all NKJV quotations must conform accurately to the NKJV text.

Any use of the NKJV text must include a proper acknowledgment as follows:

"Scripture taken from the New King James Version. Copyright © 1982 by Thomas Nelson,

Inc. Used by permission. All rights reserved."

COPYRIGHT INFORMATION

"Scripture taken from the NEW AMERICAN STANDARD BIBLE®, Copyright © 1960,1962,1963,1 968,1971,1972,1973,1975,1977,1995 by The Lockman Foundation. Used by permission."

The text of the New American Standard Bible® may be quoted and/or reprinted up to and inclusive of five hundred (500) verses without express written permission of The Lockman Foundation, providing the verses do not amount to a complete book of the Bible nor do the verses quoted account for more than 25% of the total work in which they are quoted.

Notice of copyright must appear on the title or copyright page of the work as follows:

"Scripture taken from the NEW AMERICAN STANDARD BIBLE®, Copyright © 1960,1962,1963,1968,1971,1972,1973,1975,1977,1995 by The Lockman Foundation. Used by permission."

COPYRIGHT INFORMATION

All other Scriptures are of the Author's interpretation. In addition, the scope and subject of this work is a representation of the Author's personal belief and interpretation, including all material of statements and articles included.

TABLE OF CONTENTS

COPYRIGHT INFORMATION..........................3
INTRODUCTION..9
CHAPTER 1 CROSS ROADS............................13
CHAPTER 2 CROSS ROADS OF LIFE MOST CHALLENING MOMENTS...........................43
CHAPTER 3 THE CROSS ROADS OF FAITH & BIBLE..66
CHAPTER 4 THE TURNING POINTS OF THE RAPTURE...87
CHAPTER 5 THE TURNING POINTS OF REVELATION..96
CHAPTER 6 THE TURNING POINTS OF THE TRIBULATION..104
CHAPTER 7 THE TURNING POINTS OF THE PROPHETIC TIME CLOCK..........................121
CHAPTER 8 WHERE ARE WE NOW ON THAT PROPHETIC TIME CLOCK..........................130
CHAPTER 9 THE WORLD TOMORROW.........138
CHAPTER 10 SATAN THE GOD OF THIS WORLD...158
CHAPTER 11 THE FUTURE KINGDOM OF GOD...197
CHAPTER 12 THE TURNING POINTS OF JERUSALEM...221

CHAPTER 13 BIBICAL PRINCIPLES OF PRAYERS AND WORDS..................233
CHAPTER 14 THE KEYS TO WISDOM............246
CHAPTER 15 CROWNS AND REWARDS........265

ACKNOWLEDGMENTS AND MORE ABOUT THE AUTHOR...................................273

INTRODUCTION

Cross Roads are life's Turning Points, and in this book, I interchange the two. From my point of view, the two are the same. So when you see the terms, turning points or cross roads think of them as the same thing. Cross Roads is a place where two or more of your decisions of supreme importance come to a conclusion. Turning points is the direction, or path you will follow once you come to a conclusion. You can think of these terms as this, Cross Roads, two or more streets come together, Turning Points, you could go left or right, the direction you have chosen is your Turning Point. It is important to remember that these cross roads act in opposition to each other. Moreover, they can alter your turning point and bring about an abrupt change; they do tend to be overlapping of one another. You will need to see them from God's Divine Viewpoint. To use and understand God's Divine Viewpoint you must take a systematic survey of you cross roads and turning points.

The cross roads of our lives always comes to us through our thoughts and our thoughts lead us to our turning point, this is why it is best to keep your thoughts on God. In addition, our life does act in opposition to our cross roads, life goes in many direction, and sometimes in an opposing manner to our cross roads. The cross roads of our life are a reflection on our lives and the decisions we make, our turning points. These cross roads can inspiration us or drag us to Hell…I pray that the re-life recommendations in this book will give you real-life turning points into everyday living. My hope is to offer Biblical Principle and insight into the Bible and your own cross roads, so you will experience the grace of God and be able to see His Divine Viewpoint.

In life, we are faced with cross roads that have the ability to change the way we think and act. These cross roads come to us in everything we do and have the capacity to go in many directions. No matter what cross roads we face, there is a way to make the most of them, by changing our perspective of them with the use of Scripture, and God's Divine Viewpoint. Through out this book I use Scriptures to show you the truth, but do not take my word for it search the Bible for your self. "He must indeed have a blind soul who cannot see that some great purpose and design is being worked out here below of which we have the honor to be the faithful servants." (Winston Churchill, to the United States Congress, WWII)

Every cross road starts with a defining moment, ending in a turning point. We are seeing more and more of these biblical cross roads each day. It is much too late to heed God's warning to return to him, our living God's ways. Our world will not be spared, we as human beings have reached that point-of-no return. The politicians and heads of Government have no answers for us. The Bible alone will you find advance knowledge of what is now certain to occur. As this book will demonstrate, we are now witnessing the fulfillment of numerous unique turning points or prophecies. These cross roads are setting the stage for the return of Jesus Christ.

The big question is have you reach the cross roads in your life where you believe in God? How did we reach the point of no return? Are we at that point, where it is too late to return to Gods ways? How did we arrive at this point? All are good questions to ask. In the pages that follow, you will get the answers to these questions. In fact, you may find your own cross roads that will lead you to God and our Lord and Saver Jesus Christ. I trust that this book will inform, inspire, and encourage you too personally look and study the meaning of your own cross roads and that of the Bible. At the end of the book, I share with you some of my own cross roads. To obtain the full understanding of this book please read the entire book; paying special attention to the Bible references I provide.

Thank you and God Bless

Rev.John R. Spiker
Baltimore, Maryland
February 2012

CHAPTER 1

CROSS ROADS

In life, we are faced with decisions that are cross roads! The essential aspect of these cross roads is that we have choices to make. These cross roads are in everything we do, and have the capacity to go in many directions. They have the capacity to go in the wrong direction; they also have the capacity to go in the right direction. These cross roads come in many sizes and shapes, and can be very big or small. One big problem is when we see these cross roads or our turning point, and we make our decision we often expect instant change. As with most worthwhile change, it takes time, patience, and perseverance. No matter what cross roads or turning points we face, there is a way to make the most of them, by changing our perspective of them. We do this with the biblical principles that are taught in the Bible, and by tacking a systematic survey of our turning points and cross roads. God does use cross roads to help us and we can see and understand God's power and plan for us through these turning points. My hope is to offer life giving turning points (insight) for everyday living, and for you to be able to see and understand them every day.

Every cross road starts with a defining moment. In addition, every new beginning starts with a turning point. One key to understanding them is to know how they may have had an impact in our lives. The key to Bible Scriptures is to understand how God uses cross roads and how to recognize them and which turning point to chose. God's plain for us is base on cross roads; In addition, we must understand that Satan the devil uses our cross roads to lead us astray. Satan knows prophecy and he parallels everything in the bible so he can deceive us.

We are seeing more and more of these Biblical cross roads each day now. God has giving us warnings throughout our history in prophecies, momentous warnings to those who read the Scriptures. I like to call them turning points. These Scriptures in the Bible are now our only hope. It is much too late now to heed God's warning to return to him, our living God's ways. Our world will not be spared we as human beings have reached that point-of-no return. The politicians and heads of Government have no answers for us. The Bible alone will you find advance knowledge of what is now certain to come or occur. Moreover, occur before no life is left on the Earth. We will need to have Faith in Jesus Christ in the days ahead. It is almost time for the Almighty to destroy. Prepare for the day of the Lord, That great and terrible day of His fury and anger. You should prepare yourself for the Rapture, Tribulation, and not 2012. So many people prepared for Y2K, and now 2012, but this is not what we need to be ready for.

Have you reach the cross roads in your life where you believe in God? In addition, how did we get to this point? These are good questions to ask, and the answers are found in the Bible and there are particularly striking to us because the prophets of the Bible have predicted a precise pattern of events that will fit together during this period, the end-of-days. This period is the end-of-day's turning points, a period where the anti-Jewish and Christian attitude among the world has reached a zenith. This zenith or precise pattern of events will lead to Armageddon and it will draw all nations into it. Armageddon is that great and final conflict, the last world war of history, will take place in Israel and in conjunction with the second coming of Jesus Christ our Lord and Saver.

This war is described in Daniel, Joel, Zechariah, and Revelation of the Bible. In addition, it will occur in the tribulation in the final days.

Even though the pattern of events where predicted at different times and from different places or locations they all can be identified and properly fit the prophetic scenario of events that will lead us all. This final war and the events that immediately follow Armageddon have been predicated over time. This great and final conflict is the major theme in the end-times. Every facet of prophecy in the Bible that is interpreted as occurring in the end-times, somehow relates to the great and final war and our turning points. These turning points or prophetic scenarios do not happened all at once, but over time just as they have been predicated over time.

The key to understanding the Bible's cross roads is to know the signs that will come and signal the predicted pattern of events. One key is the miraculous return and rebirth of the scattered people of Israel to their ancient homeland. This cross road was formally fulfilled May 15, 1948 and just as it was precisely predicted. Jesus Christ predicted how Jerusalem would fall by the edge of the sword, and would be led captive into all the nations, and that Jerusalem would be trampled under foot by the Gentiles until the times of the

Gentiles be fulfilled. This prophecy was just before his death. Jesus predicted the destruction and dispersion of the people who was rejecting him. Moreover, this all happened thirty-seven years after His death just as precisely as He had said. This is described in Luke 21. While Jesus was in the Temple some of his disciples began talking about the majestic stonework of the Temple and the memorial decorations on the walls so Jesus said to them "The time is coming when all these things will be completely demolished. Not one stone will be left on top of another!" Jesus also said that they the people who had rejected Him would be killed by the sword and be sent away as captives and that Jerusalem would be trampled down until the period of the Gentiles ends.

One key point in the same prophecy is the time limit on the period of Jerusalem's desolations and captivity, "Until the times of the Gentiles are fulfilled." The times of the Gentiles began to come to an end in June 1967 this is the time when the Jews recapture of Jerusalem took place. This time is fast ending; the time of the Gentiles is all most over. The Gentiles times will be completed when God sets up His promised kingdom.

The other point that we must look at is the burdensome stone for the world. Zechariah predicted that Jerusalem will become a burdensome stone for all the people and that the nations of the earth will be gathered for war because of it. As predicted by Zechariah, Jerusalem has become a burdensome stone for all peoples. Therefore, you can see how we have reached the cross road of the point of no re-turn. A great and terrible time is coming to the world and you will have to prepare for it and acquire some skills to help you. You will need to have faith and believe in Jesus Christ. In the days ahead, you will need to prepare for the day of the Lord, that great and terrible day of his fury and anger. It is a time for the Almighty to destroy. The day to destroy is the Great White Throne Judgment, and is for all who have lived throughout history regardless of their stature or position who died or still living at the time of judgment without acknowledging and accepting Jesus Christ's payment for their sins. However, before the day to destroy, there is judgment to come on the earth. You are totally unprepared if you have yet to trust in Jesus Christ, and do not come to trust in him in the days ahead. What about you love ones, are they prepare? Are you leading yourself or your love ones headlong into the tribulation? Are you preparing for the rapture? You must understand all the turning points and cross roads in the days ahead.

The tribulation is a future seven-year period of time when God will finish his discipline of Israel and His judgment on the unbelieving world. The church made up of all who has trusted in the Lord Jesus Christ to save them from being punished for sin, will not be present during the tribulation. The church will be removed from the earth in an event known as the rapture. The rapture is that time when a trumpet will sound, our Lord Jesus Christ will descend from heaven with a shout, and we who are believers in him dead or alive at that time will rise to meet him.

There is a war with Satan, and it is a battle over souls. This war is between God and Satan the devil and all humans against Satan. The more Satan can keep us from knowing about this war and the battle over souls, the better his chances of ensuring and dragging souls to hell and his fate. There are countless souls that are now in ignorance and in danger of losing there souls. Of all the deceptions Satan has use through out the ages since the Garden of Eden, getting us to believe him that he does not exists and not to fear God has been his most effective tool in this battle over souls.

Who is going to fight for souls? Who is going to warn all the lost souls? Who will give them the message that they do not have to serve Satan? Who has the faith to go into battle, serve the Lord, and win over souls? All who have faith in Jesus Christ that is who! Like it or not if you believe in God, you are in that war. There is a war, and you must choose sides. This war is a war for souls. The more Satan can keep this from people, the better are his chances of ensuring souls and dragging them to hell and his fate. The more knowledge of this war we can spread to the world, the better our possibility of assisting God in bringing souls to heaven.

We must try to get this knowledge out, and we must try to help save the souls of are love ones and all the lost souls who wander around in ignorance of God's mercy. There are countless souls that are now in ignorance and in danger of losing there souls. Of all the deceptions Satan has used through out the ages since the Garden of Eden, getting man to believe that he does not exists, and believe that we do not have to fear God, has been his most effective tools in this war. The vast majority of souls in danger are the ones who's view of Satan is, Satan who? In addition, they do not realize they are doomed to share his fate, unless they turn to God and Jesus Christ. Satan hates man (humans) and he wants to destroy as many as he can. We as humans reached the point of no returned at this time, when Satan was in the Garden of Eden.

We cannot run fast enough to hide our eyes and ears anymore from what is going on in the world, Satan's actions and statements are coming through loud and clear. Moreover, all this evil is a battle over souls. Who is going to fight for souls? Who is going to warn these people? Who will tell them the message that they do not have to serve Satan? Who has the faith to go into battle, serve the Lord, and win over souls? All who have faith in Jesus Christ that is who.

This war is upon us, whether we like it or not and there's no escaping it. Our time is short and we are faced with a decision. Either we are going to serve Satan or we will pick up the sword and fight. In addition, many will lay down their lives in the process. So the big issue is where do you stand with God? Do you know God? Do you want to know Him personally? Are you close to God, so you can talk with Him and He can talk to you? You will need God to face pure demonic power; you can stand against it with the power and authority of Jesus Christ!

Time is short we are in the last days that the bible talks about. The scriptures talk about the time of the season, know that we are in the season that Jesus gave an illustration on. The kingdom of God is near. It is imperative that we come to faith at this time in the season. That great and terrible day will be here very soon. We are to learn a lesson from the fig tree. When Luke wrote about the season he said the kingdom of God is near, but Matthew said you could know Jesus is very near. This two are the same thing because it is Jesus Christ kingdom. However, both said this generation would not pass from the scene until all the events Jesus gave will have taken place. (The generation that sees these events).And Jesus said there are signs that indicate the end is near.

Why are so many people willing to believe in 2012 end of the world Idea? Why are their so many disasters of Biblical proportions in the media these days? What is happening, can this all be biblical that is going on now? Moreover, are these cross roads? Just look at the recent media reports from around the world describing disaster as Biblical proportions. Can all this be the Biblical plagues that the scriptures talk about in the end of days?

Since the beginning, humankind has held a fascination with future events. The desire to know the future is big in this-day-and-age; just look at all the books, TV. Shows, media, New Age phenomenon, philosophers, and self-proclaimed prophets. These things are more evidenced that people want to believe in something more. My guess is in these times people are searching for something with spiritual significance, and this allows them to believe in a higher power or intelligence. Should you expect the world to end in 2012? According to today's culture yes? Nevertheless, not to the scriptures in the Bible.

The 2012 phenomenon concerning the ancient Mayans civilization is base on how they tracked the movement of the stars and planets. They developed the Mesoamerican calendar, a method to keep track of time. A sophisticated method that is beyond my scope to understand. However, what exactly is supposed to happen on December 21, 2012 remains a raging debate. The end calls for natural disasters as earthquakes, tsunamis, typhoons, solar storms, and asteroid or comet to collide with the earth. Is all these events enough for you to say, the end is here? Do you think there are biblical? Is there any truth that the end will come in 2012?

I say with absolute certainty, that these are not the biblical plagues that are going to end the world. I say with absolute certainty 2012 is not the end of the world. I am not saying that these are not biblical plagues, just not the end ones, and I am not saying nothing of significance will happen, but it will not be the end on December 21, 2012. However, they can be turning points for us, as the year 2012 approaches with media attention and even panic.

Are you looking for reassuring, or do you find comfort in knowing that such events are historically and not that uncommon, like the weather, disease, polluting, and the domes-day-Sayers. Is all this prompting you to theorize that they may be signs of the times as the bible has said? Are you shrugging these events off to natural happenstance? On the other hand, are you looking for something like the truth? Are you thinking it is time to begin your own investigation? Perhaps you just have a feeling (sick-sense) or concerns about there is nothing to see here a conspiracy to you. Is the nothing to see here the safe and middle of the road explanation, the way out for you? The nothing to see here conspiracy is nothing out of the ordinary perhaps, but another look might be in order. It is easy to dismiss these events, if you remain unconvinced at this time what should you be doing? You should be getting answers by asking direct and thoughtful questions, instead of relying on anecdotal evidence from who knows whom, in addition, looking for cross roads.

When 2012 comes and goes, you will live on and still be looking. While our planet will not be destroyed, the end is near. The world as we know it will end. We do live in the end times. Jesus Christ is coming he will conquer the enemies of God and establish his kingdom for 1,000 years.

If you are looking for a higher power or intelligence there is good news, there is one and he does exist in the person of Jesus Christ, thank God. You want to know when this age is coming to an end, and where Jesus is coming. How is going to set up a kingdom for 1,000 years? You say when will all these things be. The truth is we cannot possible know the day nor the hour of Jesus Christ return, and we dare not set a date for it. Only God knows the day and time, but we do know he is coming and what we should be doing. We should be looking for cross roads and turning points, and reading the Scriptures in the Bible. So he is coming but we don't know when, why be concern, or even be alarmed over it? Why should we be prepared are all good questions? We do not know the time or day, but we do know the season and the signs of the times, (the turning points) all we have to do is look at the illustration Jesus gave concerning the fig tree "when the leaves come out, you know without being told that summer is near." Some of Jesus disciples questioning him privately ask, "When will these things be, and what will be the sign." In addition, we know the turning points have predicted a precise Patten of events that will fit it all together.

How can I be absolute certainty 2012 is not the end, by the word of God through the Bible, it has proven it's credibility of foretelling the future, hundreds of bible prophecies have come true, with 100% accuracy, and there is prophecies yet to be fulfilled. You can bet the house on it that these future events will be fulfilled with 100% accuracy to. In today's world, there is plenty to be alarmed about whether it is crime, war, terrorism, or natural disaster and numerous other reasons. We have good cause for alarm, what is more alarming is the lack of preparedness for Jesus Christ and his kingdom, and looking for turning points that can help us to understand what is going on.

We do not know the day, but we do know the season, and we know Jesus gave us a warring to watch and pray, so we would be worthy to escape these things. You see there is a great and terrible day coming. Therefore, when some takes exception to us who are watching, all they need to know is we do it because we are commended to by Jesus Christ.

When the Lord does come for his church will you be prepare. If not you will not be going anywhere but into the tribulation. That will be a time in the world, that has never occurred since the beginning of time nor never shall be. You will be left on the earth to go through the tribulation. Perhaps you are one of those

# Understanding Your Cross Roads with God's Divine Viewpoint 27

who just are not concerned about it because you are a good person and you think everything will be all right in the end. Alternatively, you might think that good people do not have to go through the tribulation or there will not be one. To be good and not believe in Jesus Christ is very wrong, with out faith in Jesus you will have to go through the tribulation no matter how good you think you might have been. There is good news for the people of the rapture there judgment is for reward, but The Great White Throne Judgment is for death, and will come only after the rapture and tribulation and the 1,000 years reign of Christ is over!

You can live with wonderful expectations or live in fear. The world as we know it is rapidly coming to an end, make the short time left to come to God. By faith, you can make a decision for God, and the turning points can guide you. There are deceiving spirits among us to lead astray. As long as they are out there, things will only get worse. Nevertheless, do not let it get to you; stick with the word of God. You will need the word to avoid the deceiving spirits and the devil. Remember the Devil will use turning points against you.

Yes, all have sin and fall short, short of the glory of God. There is a way out of sin and it is not by being a good person, your salvation is not a reward for the good you have done. You cannot boast and say look at what I have done, and now I will be going to heaven. God is going to save me for I am a very good person; no this is not the way. God will save you when you have faith in Jesus Christ. It is only by God's special favor that you can be saved. Therefore, there is no way you can take credit for it. For it is by grace of the Father and a free gift from God. The scriptures say that God heard you at just the right time when you repented, on the day of salvation he helped you and indeed is ready to help you right now. The day of salvation is any day one repents. For today is the day of salvation.

The right time, you see there is a right time for Jesus to come. God has been giving us all time to trust in him, we should realize how kind, tolerant, and patient he has been with us. Time to turn from sin there will be no judgment for those who trust in him. However, you will be storing up terrible punishment for yourselves if you do not have faith; those who trust in God and believe that Jesus is the son of God and that he paid the price for are sins have been made right with the Lord.

Your wages for the work that you do are not free, you have earn what you have receive, so it will be this way on judgment day, you will earn what you receive.

Your good deeds will not earn you faith, it was not Abraham good deeds that God accepted him, it was that he believed what God had said and was declared righteous by his faith. Faith is a gift from God all you have to do is ask, and what joy for those who ask and there sins are forgiven and put out of sight, yes what joy for those whose sin no longer are counted against them by the Lord

The scriptures, tells us God spoke to our ancestors in many ways and times and has showed many turning points, but now in these final days he is using his son Jesus Christ. The final days are here, and the end of the age is here and was in progress during Christ ministry, and is in full swing now. The last days will continue until Jesus returns for the judgment, the day of the Lord, that great and terrible day.

So why not come to faith? Before that great and terrible day arrives. Remember we are in the season and we are seeing more and more turning points. Why not come to faith now and receive eternal live, and this way you will go in the rapture, and will not go through the tribulation time on earth. If a person does not repent, God will prepare his deadly weapons against them. God does warn the wicked saying "you are under the penalty of death" you will die in yours sins if you refuse to repent and ask Jesus to come into your life. If you will turn from you sins, none of them will be brought up again. You will surely live. Therefore, if a good person turns to evil, he will die, but if the wicked person turns to God and repents, they will live. Sinners have no place among the godly. God will not let the wicked go unpunished. The penalty for any sin is death.

The path of the wicked leads to destruction, to satisfy God's anger. The bible says God is slow to anger yes, but he still has anger for the wicked that is all who have sinned. The bible also says God is rich in unfailing love forgiving every kind of sin, and rebellion. Even so, God will arouse his anger against evil and sin. God has punished Israel so many times because of all her sins and arousing his anger. We can see God's anger and punishment in (1Kings), Baaha, and his son Elah led Israel to commit sin with their idols, arousing the anger of God. In addition, we see how the Lords anger did not come against Israel during Hezekiah's lifetime, because he Hezekiah repented of his pride and the people of Jerusalem humbled themselves in (2Chronicles).

In the last days, there will be scoffers, who will laugh and not remember. On the other hand, understand what the prophets said long ago, and not understand or see these cross roads, or what God has commended us to do. They will laugh at the truth and do any evil they desire. There argument will be then where is Jesus, did he not promised to come back and get you so you would be with him, ok where is he? They will say everything is the same and is going to remain the same. He is not coming back and he will not take you to where he is. These scoffers have deliberately forget about how God made the heavens and everything in it, but on judgment day God will consumed all ungodly people and they will perish.

A word to the scoffers and all ungodly people, you see Jesus is not slow in his return as you might thing. He is benign patient with us for our sake. God is giving us all more time for us to repent and have faith in Jesus Christ. Nevertheless, that day will come, the day of the Lord Jesus Christ, that great and terrible day. It will come as unexpectedly as a thief will. On that day, the heavens will pass away with a terrible noise, and everything in them will disappear in fire. Everything will come into judgment. What these scoffers refuse to believe is they Jesus Christ came to save us and that he will return to judge us. The Bible says the day will surely come when God, will judge everyone's secret life by Jesus Christ. Neither their silver nor gold shall be able to save them in the day of the Lord. That great and terrible day of the Lord is near, it is near and hastens quickly because the Lord is bitter and he will bring distress upon the whole earth. Because of sin, blood will be poured out like dust, and flesh shall be like trash.

The Lord will gather the armies of the world into the valley of Jehoshaphat, there he will judge them. This is what the scriptures say in the Bible. The scriptures say if you obey his commands with purity, no one can find fault with you, from the time you obey the father until Jesus returns. He will return on judgment day, that great and terrible day. But there is good news for believers in Jesus Christ on that day, those who fear the Lord that there is a scroll of remembrance written for them There is a scroll of remembrance for those who fear the Lord and love to thing about him. The Lord says "They will be my people on the day when I act; they will be my own special treasure. I will spare them as a father spares an obedient and dutiful child, then you will see the deference between the righteous and the wicked, between those serve God and those who do not." The obedient child is one who obeys the father, and the dutiful is one is motivated by sense of duty.

One of Satan's most effective tools was getting us to believe him that we do not have to fear God. Somehow, we have come to believe the concept that God is sitting up in heaven, He will refuse us nothing, and He will not discipline us His children. That

God is all compassion and loving and we can do no wrong. The concept we do not have to fear God is all wrong. God does not have the same emotions as us humans. In addition, He does not have the emotions and thoughts we are found of attributing to Him. We are so concerned about feelings we hesitate to share the truth about God, because of the fear of offending someone.

We humans something refuse to discipline our children because of emotions and we do not want upset them and cause ourselves more pain and difficulties. We like to think this why because we assume God has the same emotions as we do. We do not fear the Lord just as children don' fear the parents who does not discipline them. Moreover, because we have no idea of His power and greatness or of His thoughts. However, God does discipline His children and we should fear Him.

Do you suppose God will let us all into heaven with our sins? Why do we thing that God is tolerating are sins? Our Lord Is a God of justice and mercy, but He does not tolerate sin. We do have a wonderful God, He does love us all and is tolerate of us and He knows the end from the beginning, and He knew Satan would cause sin.

If we deliberately continue sinning after we have received knowledge of the truth, there is no longer any sacrifice that will cover these sins. There will be only fear of the Lord's revenge, and how He will judge us. In addition, the raging fire that will consume His enemies. It will be a terrible thing to fall into the hands of the Lord over sin. If the demons tremble in terror of God, who do we think we do not have to? Because Satan has tricked us into believing, we do not have to. The Serpent was the shrewdest of all the creatures God made. The Devil is so cunning and shrewd that he tricked us humans into sin.

Do not give the Devil the opportunity to tempt you. He needs a reason to do so, he prowls around looking for an opportunity. Do not give him the change to tempt you. Watch out for attacks from the Devil he is looking for some victim to devour. To resist the devil you must make a spiritual renewal of you thoughts and attitudes. Throw off your old evil nature and former way of life. You must have a new nature because you are a new person you know you were created in God's likeness.

Satan used every tactic he can to discourage us. Satan and his demons always know how to hit where it hurts the most. They have had more than 6,000 years of practice on us humans. They know are natures very well by now, and they most certainly know how easily we get discouraged when we do not get our way. We are under continually temptation to escape from the reality of the world. Moreover, there are so many whys to escape, we can used the TV by turning off our minds. Many people used drugs or sex to escape and another great temptation is to escape into a fantasy world, living in a world that is not real and one that draws us further away from God. New age techniques also help us to escape reality.

Instead of escaping from reality, we must live in it and we must discipline our minds to think about God. We must think about the scriptures and talk to the Lord. We need to evaluate what is happening to us and around us in the light of the Bible. God's word is our source of wisdom and guidance in this world. As we do this, we will find that the Holy Spirit will speak to us more and more frequently. Then no matter what is happening around us we know that God is near.

We must seek the Lord now so when trouble does come into are lives we will have the relationship we need with God that will help us during our time of need. Do not let your natural desires stop you from obtaining God's precious gifts and His treasure, the treasure of knowing Him. Many times the Lord will hold back from answering us because He wants us to seek Him more earnestly. Do not think that He does not hear you, you must learn to wait on the Lord. Sometimes are emotions are so intense that they block us from hearing the Lord. Accept it, whatever the Lord does, you must just ask Him for help, and He will do the rest. We must talk to God, not just ask Him for things. Most people do not know how to just talk with God, but He does desire a fellowship with us. Let God be a part of your everyday life, so as you go about your daily life and activities start thinking and talking to God. The Lord is interested in us, yes even the smallest details and everything we do. Nothing is to boring or insignificant for Him. God will give is undivided attention. Live according to the spirit, by keeping your mind on God.

Yes, God does know all things, and He is all loving and carrying. However, this does bring up an important point. If God is all-loving, why does God take little children to heaven? Moreover, why does God answer some prayers and not others? Why… because of His whys! God said "My thoughts are nothing like your thoughts," and His ways are far beyond anything we can imagine.

We must always seek to do the Lords will, look at the Lords prayer…Thy will be done on earth as it is in heaven and remember what Jesus said Father you will be done and not mine. Sometimes God gives people their request because of their continued pleading, when the thing they are asking for is not actually, what is best. For instance, the sick child, when perhaps God wants to take them home to prevent the child intense suffers in the future, or from falling away from Him in the future. There is a story in scriptures that we should study soberly and prayerfully. It is an example of asking God for what is not the best thing for us; it should always be God's will for us. The story is about Hezekiah and how he served the Lord faithfully during his life time, and how he became ill. The Lord said to put his house in order for he was going to die. Nevertheless, he prayed and the Lord heard his prayer, and did as he had asked. However, this was not the best thing for him it was not God's will but Hezekiah that he should live.

{2 Kings 20:1-21 NLT}-[1] about that time Hezekiah became deathly ill, and the prophet Isaiah son of Amoz went to visit him. He gave the king this message: "This is what the LORD says: Set your affairs in order, for you are going to die. You will not recover from this illness." [2] When Hezekiah heard this, he turned his face to the wall and prayed to the LORD, [3] "Remember, O LORD, how I have always been faithful to you and have served you single-mindedly, always doing what pleases you." Then he broke down and wept bitterly. [4] But before Isaiah had left the middle courtyard, this message came to him from the

LORD: [5] "Go back to Hezekiah, the leader of my people. Tell him, 'This is what the LORD, the God of your ancestor David, says: I have heard your prayer and seen your tears. I will heal you, and three days from now you will get out of bed and go to the Temple of the LORD. [6] I will add fifteen years to your life, and I will rescue you and this city from the king of Assyria. I will defend this city for my own honor and for the sake of my servant David.'" [7] Then Isaiah said, "Make an ointment from figs." So Hezekiah's servants spread the ointment over the boil, and Hezekiah recovered! [8] Meanwhile, Hezekiah had said to Isaiah, "What sign will the LORD give to prove that he will heal me and that I will go to the Temple of the LORD three days from now?" [9] Isaiah replied, "This is the sign from the LORD to prove that he will do as he promised. Would you like the shadow on the sundial to go forward ten steps or backward ten steps?" [10] "The shadow always moves forward," Hezekiah replied, "so that would be easy. Make it go ten steps backward instead." [11] So Isaiah the prophet asked the LORD to do this, and he caused the shadow to move ten steps backward on the sundial of Ahaz! [12] Soon after this, Merodach-baladan son of Baladan, king of Babylon, sent Hezekiah his best wishes and a gift, for he had heard that Hezekiah had been very sick. [13] Hezekiah received the Babylonian envoys and showed them everything in his treasure-houses—

the silver, the gold, the spices, and the aromatic oils. He also took them to see his armory and showed them everything in his royal treasuries! There was nothing in his palace or kingdom that Hezekiah did not show them. [14] Then Isaiah the prophet went to King Hezekiah and asked him, "What did those men want? Where were they from?" Hezekiah replied, "They came from the distant land of Babylon." [15] "What did they see in your palace?" Isaiah asked. "They saw everything," Hezekiah replied. "I showed them everything I own—all my royal treasuries." [16] Then Isaiah said to Hezekiah, "Listen to this message from the LORD: [17] The time is coming when everything in your palace—all the treasures stored up by your ancestors until now—will be carried off to Babylon. Nothing will be left, says the LORD. [18] Some of your very own sons will be taken away into exile. They will become eunuchs who will serve in the palace of Babylon's king." [19] Then Hezekiah said to Isaiah, "This message you have given me from the LORD is good." For the king was thinking, "At least there will be peace and security during my lifetime." [20] The rest of the events in Hezekiah's reign, including the extent of his power and how he built a pool and dug a tunnel to bring water into the city, are recorded in The Book of the History of the Kings of Judah. [21] Hezekiah died, and his son Manasseh became the next king.

{2 Kings 21:1-25 NLT}-[1] Manasseh was twelve years old when he became king, and he reigned in Jerusalem fifty-five years. His mother was Hephzibah. [2] He did what was evil in the LORD's sight, following the detestable practices of the pagan nations that the LORD had driven from the land ahead of the Israelites. [3] He rebuilt the pagan shrines his father, Hezekiah, had destroyed. He constructed altars for Baal and set up an Asherah pole, just as King Ahab of Israel had done. He also bowed before all the powers of the heavens and worshiped them. [4] He built pagan altars in the Temple of the LORD, the place where the LORD had said, "My name will remain in Jerusalem forever." [5] He built these altars for all the powers of the heavens in both courtyards of the LORD's Temple. [6] Manasseh also sacrificed his own son in the fire. He practiced sorcery and divination, and he consulted with mediums and psychics. He did much that was evil in the LORD's sight, arousing his anger. [7] Manasseh even made a carved image of Asherah and set it up in the Temple, the very place where the LORD had told David and his son Solomon: "My name will be honored forever in this Temple and in Jerusalem—the city I have chosen from among all the tribes of Israel. [8] If the Israelites will be careful to obey my commands—all the laws my servant Moses gave them—I will not send them into exile from this land that I gave their ancestors." [9] But the people refused to listen, and Manasseh led them to do even more evil than the pagan nations that the LORD had destroyed when the people of Israel entered the land. [10] Then the LORD said through his servants the prophets: [11] "King Manasseh of Judah has done many detestable things. He is even more wicked than the Amorites, who lived in this land before Israel. He has caused the people of Judah to sin with his idols. [12] So this is what the LORD, the God of Israel, says: I will bring such disaster on Jerusalem and Judah that the ears of those who hear about it will tingle with horror. [13] I will judge Jerusalem by the same standard I used for Samaria and the same measure I used for the family of Ahab. I will wipe away the people of Jerusalem as one wipes a dish and turns it upside down. [14] Then I will reject even the remnant of my own people who are left, and I will hand them over as plunder for their enemies. [15] For they have done great evil in my sight and have angered me ever since their ancestors came out of Egypt." [16] Manasseh also murdered many innocent people until Jerusalem was filled from one end to the other with innocent blood. This was in addition to the sin that he caused the people of Judah to commit, leading them to do evil in the LORD's sight. [17] The rest of the events in Manasseh's reign and everything he did, including the sins he committed, are recorded in The

Book of the History of the Kings of Judah. [18] When Manasseh died, he was buried in the palace garden, the garden of Uzza. Then his son Amon became the next king. [19] Amon was twenty-two years old when he became king, and he reigned in Jerusalem two years. His mother was Meshullemeth, the daughter of Haruz from Jotbah. [20] He did what was evil in the LORD's sight, just as his father, Manasseh, had done. [21] He followed the example of his father, worshiping the same idols his father had worshiped. [22] He abandoned the LORD, the God of his ancestors, and he refused to follow the LORD's ways. [23] Then Amon's own officials conspired against him and assassinated him in his palace. [24] But the people of the land killed all those who had conspired against King Amon, and they made his son Josiah the next king. [25] The rest of the events in Amon's reign and what he did are recorded in The Book of the History of the Kings of Judah.

Can you see how God was going to take Hezekiah home because he knew the future and all the evil that would result if Hezekiah continued to live? So we should learn to seek the will of the Lord. We should not be so quick to assume we know what is best, and even demand of God what we want. Moreover, assuming that we know more than God, in any situation.

CHAPTER 2

CROSS ROADS OF LIFE MOST CHALLENING MOMENTS

Our Cross Roads makes a profound difference in our lives! With God's help and love, we can discover the deeper meaning of life most challenging moments. Through cross roads, God does show us the hidden meaning of life, or to say His will for us. God teaches us cross roads in the Bible, through the Scriptures our cross roads shows us the path to truth and peace. God's cross roads teaches us how to accept the course of our lives, and to become more reliant on Him. Moreover, to be less fearful in the face of every challenge we are faced with. God wants us to see how He uses everything in our lives for our good. God does use our turning points that we are faced with that seem inexplicable, unjust or even cruel…These events can shatter our perception of the world, understanding of ourselves, and faith in God. Remember Satan will use our cross roads against us. This is why you should take every cross road you come to, to God to see if it is the right path for you to take; we must consult the Lord on everything.

God uses the Bible Scriptures, Biblical Cross Roads, to help us understand the principles behind our turning points. In addition, He uses the Bible as a tool so we can grasp the true meaning in everything. God has giving us prophecy to use as turning points, so we can use prophecy and our current events and that of what is to come, and to see how we made it to this point, the point-of-no return. These prophecies give us solid guidelines for accurately interpreting our turning points, and the events to come. By interpret the Bible we will discover turning points of the rapture, the second coming of Christ, and the millennial Kingdom and much more.

Can it by true that everything happens for a reason? Our friends and family are fond of saying it. It sometimes is offer as comfort, a simple phrase with a big meaning. The truth is we make the decisions, but no matter what happens to us God can use it so something valuable will come out of it. Even the worst thing that can happen to you, and I had my share—there are wonderful things, hidden gifts, and opportunities for life enhancing moments. In addition, sometimes we could not have gotten them any other way; because we have missed, God's cross roads for us.

Sometimes the last thing we needed in life will happen, just at the right time but we do not see it at first. Because we were to upset to understand that it was a cross road. It was exactly what we needing. Now it was God saying, if you will not do my will, move in the direction I want, I have to do it for you. I want to reassure you, I know first hand, that when you discover the true meaning of your cross roads in your life, everything changes. You learn to wait on God; you sense that everything has meaning, that there is purpose and value in it all. With God's help, you now see how everything connects to God's will.

In addition, you see how your life is more then just a mere crap shot, it is not the roll of the dice. Now you can see how if life cross roads have no meaning, then everything is random, anything can happen. Yes, it is very painful not knowing why you get sick, or the lost of a love one, seemingly without any rhyme or reason.

However, God's ways are not ours. You might think no one else can be as stupid or unlucky as you are. The problem you face is how you can move forward. You can do this by God's Divine Viewpoint. When things happen in our lives that are so painful, it is no wonder we have trouble finding their meaning, and sometimes we will give up looking, and this can be a big mistake. You must ask God to help, many things happen to us that can challenge our faith. You get seriously ill at the worst possible moment, you think you have found the job of your dreams but something goes haywire in the first week on the job, now you have no job. You had one of those whacky childhoods and you screw up most of the time. We all have to endure many trials; Jesus told us so that we would have peace, also He said to take heart because He overcame the world. We are to be truly glad because there is wonderful joy ahead. These trials are to show that our faith is genuine and that it will remain strong.

God uses our trials for our own good; many will be purified and cleansed by there trials. The reward for trusting God will be the salvation of our souls. The good that comes out the bad things that happen will lead us to God. Sometimes the reason something happens to us is to make something better in our future. Circumstances often take us in other places, or we just plain go in the wrong direction and drift further away. This will cause God to act and shove in our faces what His will for us is, or what He wants us to be doing.

{John 16:33 NLT}-[33] I have told you all this so that you may have peace in me. Here on earth you will have many trials and sorrows. But take heart, because I have overcome the world."

{1 Peter 1:6-7 NLT}-[6] So be truly glad. There is wonderful joy ahead, even though you have to endure many trials for a little while. [7] These trials will show that your faith is genuine. It is being tested as fire tests and purifies gold—though your faith is far more precious than mere gold. So when your faith remains strong through many trials, it will bring you much praise and glory and honor on the day when Jesus Christ is revealed to the whole world.

{Daniel 12:10 NLT}-[10] Many will be purified, cleansed, and refined by these trials. But the wicked will continue in their wickedness, and none of them will understand. Only those who are wise will know what it means.

Having understanding of the true meaning of your cross roads in your life is more important than you might think or imagined. When you do not have understanding, you fail to grasp cross roads are a gift from God. A turning point can come along that teaches us whom we really are, and then makes discovering our true selves truly possible. On the surface, we have complete identities of our selves, and then we are faced with a cruel cross road that wakes us up to the fact that we truly do not know ourselves.

Why is it so hard for us to become the person we were meant to be? It is because Satan has had a hand in it all.

We go through some painful cross roads and realize the reason we went through it was that God was giving us a way to see his will for us. Our cross roads with life journey can take us over troubled waters. Nevertheless, God wants us to understand our cross roads so that we will realize we do not have to do it alone or the hard way. However, God does use are journey in life to reveal His will for us. God does aloud us to have choices, but His will for us will be done.

Sometimes God's will is done without us even realizing it; this is the good side of your turning points. When we discover the truth about our turning points in our lives, it is always to complete our growth with God. Once you see that the reason something happened was so you could walk with God, and so you could see His will for you. You will have the beginning of understanding…God's Divine Viewpoint, it is imperative that every individual knows and understands there true cross roads and how to use the ones in the Bible for the days ahead.

All we have to do to see God's Divine Viewpoint in our lives is to look in the Scriptures. In addition, to take a look at Joseph and his brothers. After Joseph brothers sold him into slavery, Joseph interpreted the dreams of Pharaoh—that there would be seven good years, followed by seven years of famine, and as for two similar dreams, means that God had decreed them and soon will make them happen. Pharaoh appointed Joseph to take the necessary measures so that they would be ready for the famine. Pharaoh said to Joseph, "I hereby put you in charge of the entire land of Egypt."

The Lord led Joseph and he proved himself an excellent servant to Pharaoh and became rich and powerful in Egypt second in all the land. Joseph prudent actions in building up stores of grain in the good years staved off the effects of the famine. In Canaan, meanwhile the famine hit hard, the land of his father, Jacob. Jacob just like Abraham had done years before, set out for Egypt to find help. Now this is how Joseph's brothers becomes intertwined with Joseph's rise to power. Joseph father Jacob sends ten of his sons, Joseph brothers to Egypt for grain from the Egyptian storehouses. The brothers get to Egypt and meet with a Great official, who is Joseph. The brothers do not realize who he is. Joseph was at least twenty years older, and speaks through an interpreter, but Joseph recognizes them. Now Joseph has a plain to reunite his entire family, he wants them to share in his good fortune of wealth and position.

Joseph planned a trick and plays a game with his brothers; this increases the suspense before the eventual happy conclusion. Joseph, being a godly man, forgave his brothers for selling him into slavery and invited all his relatives to move to Egypt, saving them from the five years of famine still to come. All of "The Children of Israel," which they were known as, moved to Egypt, which would one day enslave them, just as God had foretold Abraham. They settled in a place called Goshen, there under the protection of Joseph they flourished.

Joseph realizes the reason he went through his turning points, and he saw the will of God for him in them. He saw and understood his turning points were for his own good and the good of his family. Joseph said, "I am Joseph, your brother, whom you sold into slavery in Egypt. But do not be upset, and do not be angry with yourselves for selling me to this place. God sent me here ahead of you to preserve your lives."

{Genesis 45:7-8 NLT}-[7] God has sent me ahead of you to keep you and your families alive and to preserve many survivors. [8] So it was God who sent me here, not you! And he is the one who made me an adviser to Pharaoh—the manager of his entire palace and the governor of all Egypt.

We can look at Moses and the Exodus out of Egypt; to see how the Israelite missed God's Devine Viewpoint and how they did not understand them as cross roads. The Hebrews were finally out of Egypt after four centuries. When the people saw the mighty power that the Lord had unleashed against the Egyptians they were filled with awe. Moreover, they put their faith in the Lord. However, it did not take long for the people to complained and turned against Moses. Soon after their rescue from Egypt, the Hebrews complained to Moses, saying, "you brought us out into the wilderness to die. We have no water and we have no food." Showing great mercy, the Lord responded to their doubt by bringing them water. Moreover, He said, "Watch, I will rain bread from heaven for you; and you shall go out every morning and gather it." The Israelites could gather it and make into bread; little did they realize that they would have to live on that manna for forty years. In the third month of their exodus, the Hebrews came to the desert of Sinai and camped before Mount Sinai. God spoke to Moses, telling him that he would now give him the Laws of his Covenant.

Read the Scriptures below to see if you can find God's cross roads and His will for Abram (Abraham) and how Abraham understood God's Devine Viewpoint.

Genesis 12:1-4, 11-20 NASB}-[1] Now the LORD said to Abram, "Go forth from your country, And from your relatives And from your father's house, To the land which I will show you; [2] And I will make you a great nation, And I will bless you, And make your name great; And so you shall be a blessing;
[3] And I will bless those who bless you, And the one who curses you I will curse. And in you all the families of the earth will be blessed." [4] So Abram went forth as the LORD had spoken to him; and Lot went with him. Now Abram was seventy-five years old when he departed from Haran…[11] It came about when he came near to Egypt, that he said to Sarai his wife, "See now, I know that you are a beautiful woman; [12] and when the Egyptians see you, they will say, 'This is his wife'; and they will kill me, but they will let you live. [13] "Please say that you are my sister so that it may go well with me because of you, and that I may live on account of you." [14] It came about when Abram came into Egypt, the Egyptians saw that the woman was very beautiful. [15] Pharaoh's officials saw her and praised her to Pharaoh; and the woman was taken into Pharaoh's house. [16] Therefore he

treated Abram well for her sake; and gave him sheep and oxen and donkeys and male and female servants and female donkeys and camels. [17] But the LORD struck Pharaoh and his house with great plagues because of Sarai, Abram's wife. [18] Then Pharaoh called Abram and said, "What is this you have done to me? Why did you not tell me that she was your wife? [19] "Why did you say, 'She is my sister,' so that I took her for my wife? Now then, here is your wife, take her and go." [20] Pharaoh commanded his men concerning him; and they escorted him away, with his wife and all that belonged to him.

Abraham did not ask God why he had to go forth from his country, to some land that God would show him. And at the good old age of seventy-five. Abraham did have a weak moment in faith, he ask his wife to say that she was is sister. Now God used this moment of weakness for Abrahams own good. Abraham was treated well, so when he was escorted away he was very rich in livestock, silver and gold.

{Genesis 22:1-2 NASB}-[1] Now it came about after these things, that God tested Abraham, and said to him, "Abraham!" And he said, "Here I am." [2] He said, "Take now your son, your only son, whom you love, Isaac, and go to the land of Moriah, and offer him there as a burnt offering on one of the mountains of which I will tell you."

These scriptures show that when Abraham was tested by God this time his faith was strong. Abraham obeyed God and did not withhold even his son. Abraham understood God's Devine Viewpoint. Moreover, do you see the turning point in how God provided him a ram? The bible provides a wealth of advice to apply to our spiritual lives.

Much of that knowledge is from other people's trails and failures and there turning points. Look at the followers of Moses and what happened to them and how they reacted. God guided all of them with a cloud that move ahead of them in the daytime and a pillar of fire at night. That way they could travel whether it was day or night. He brought them through the water of the sea to dry ground, he give them miraculous food and water, yet after all this they still crave evil and sinned. They did not see these events as turning points or God's will for them God allow these events to happened as a warning to us so we would not crave evil things. God used this to teach them to get on the path. God used what had happen to them as turning points, and he used these turning points to put them on the right path again.

How does God use cross roads? What cross roads are in the Bible? These are just a few questions that are asked. Jesus told us about our trails and if we look at our trails, we will see cross roads. Cross roads, can be a push in the right direction, or just a gut felling about something. They can be very painful or full of happiness. Cross roads are prophecies, and most prophecies have been fulfilled, so we will be looking for the predicted prophecies or turning points to come, like the Rapture, tribulation Antichrist and the covenant for seven years for peace and much more.

Nevertheless, you will need to have faith to see and understand cross roads as prophecies, and to understand your own person cross roads. You can have faith as small as a mustard seed, but you can move mountains with this kind of faith. Jesus said faith could begin in very small quantity. Life, of course, is full of problems. Jesus Christ life was full of problems we could not even imagine. Yet His story is the greatest one of faith. Jesus story is not a story of unbroken success, not a story of broken spirit or of trouble and it is definitely not one of defeat.

Faith guarantees no easy way of life, but it overcomes the world. Jesus told us that we could have His peace in everything, yes even in our trials and sorrows. By living with Jesus Christ peace, it will bring us to God and His will and plan for us. Faith comes in believing, and believing comes from conversion, yes-Christian conversion faith in Jesus Christ. What exactly do I mean by conversion, I have been told it comes from a Latin word meaning to turn or change. So we can use turning points to help us find faith, and to change our ways and thoughts. God does not always operate through neat patterns in showing us our turning points. Jesus said" the wind blows where it wills, you hear the sound of it, but you do not know where it comes from or where it is going. Faith and turning points are like the wind. God has a higher ability to see the overall picture that we could never fully understand, until the day of the rapture. In addition, God has a higher ability to see what we cannot. More on this in chapter 13 biblical principles of prayers and words.

King David's son, who ruled in Jerusalem, wrote everything is meaningless, "utterly Meaningless" As you read this you will be able to understand the truth, you will see the truth is a gift from God. People who understand the truth rarely look with sorrow on the past for God has given them reason for joy in everything, which indeed is a gift from God.

{Ecclesiastes 1:1-18 NLT}-[1] These are the words of the Teacher, King David's son, who ruled in Jerusalem. [2] "Everything is meaningless," says the Teacher, "completely meaningless!" [3] What do people get for all their hard work under the sun? [4] Generations come and generations go, but the earth never changes. [5] The sun rises and the sun sets, then hurries around to rise again. [6] The wind blows south, and then turns north. Around and around it goes, blowing in circles. [7] Rivers run into the sea, but the sea is never full. Then the water returns again to the rivers and flows out again to the sea. [8] Everything is wearisome beyond description. No matter how much we see, we are never satisfied. No matter how much we hear, we are not content. [9] History merely repeats itself. It has all been done before. Nothing under the sun is truly new. [10] Sometimes people say, "Here is something new!" But actually it is old; nothing is ever truly new. [11] We don't remember what happened in the past, and in future generations, no one will remember what we are doing now. [12] I, the Teacher, was king of Israel, and I lived in Jerusalem. [13] I devoted myself to search for understanding and to explore by wisdom everything being done under heaven. I soon discovered that God has dealt a tragic existence to the human race.

[14] I observed everything going on under the sun, and really, it is all meaningless—like chasing the wind. [15] What is wrong cannot be made right. What is missing cannot be recovered. [16] I said to myself,

"Look, I am wiser than any of the kings who ruled in Jerusalem before me. I have greater wisdom and knowledge than any of them." [17] So I set out to learn everything from wisdom to madness and folly. But I learned firsthand that pursuing all this is like chasing the wind. [18] The greater my wisdom, the greater my grief. To increase knowledge only increases sorrow.

{Ecclesiastes 2:1-26 NLT}-[1] I said to myself, "Come on, let's try pleasure. Let's look for the 'good things' in life." But I found that this, too, was meaningless. [2] So I said, "Laughter is silly. What good does it do to seek pleasure?" [3] After much thought, I decided to cheer myself with wine. And while still seeking wisdom, I clutched at foolishness. In this way, I tried to experience the only happiness most people find during their brief life in this world. [4] I also tried to find meaning by building huge homes for myself and by planting beautiful vineyards. [5] I made gardens and parks, filling them with all kinds of fruit trees. [6] I built reservoirs to collect the water to irrigate my many flourishing groves. [7] I bought slaves, both men and women, and others were born into my household. I also owned large herds and flocks, more than any of the kings who had lived in Jerusalem before me. [8] I collected great sums of silver and gold, the treasure of many kings and provinces. I hired wonderful singers, both men and women, and had many beautiful concubines. I had everything a man could desire! [9] So I became greater than all who had lived in Jerusalem before me, and my wisdom never failed me. [10] Anything I wanted, I would take. I denied myself no pleasure. I even found great pleasure in hard work, a reward for all my labors. [11] But as I looked at everything I had worked so hard to accomplish, it was all so meaningless—like chasing the wind. There was nothing really worthwhile anywhere. [12] So I decided to compare wisdom with foolishness and madness (for who can do this better than I, the king?). [13] I thought, "Wisdom is better than foolishness, just as light is better than darkness.

[14] For the wise can see where they are going, but fools walk in the dark." Yet I saw that the wise and the foolish share the same fate. [15] Both will die. So I said to myself, "Since I will end up the same as the fool, what's the value of all my wisdom? This is all so meaningless!" [16] For the wise and the foolish both die. The wise will not be remembered any longer than the fool. In the days to come, both will be forgotten. [17] So I came to hate life because everything done here under the sun is so troubling. Everything is meaningless—like chasing the wind. [18] I came to hate all my hard work here on earth, for I must leave to others everything I have earned. [19] And who can tell whether my successors will be wise or foolish? Yet they will control everything I have gained by my skill

and hard work under the sun. How meaningless! [20] So I gave up in despair, questioning the value of all my hard work in this world. [21] Some people work wisely with knowledge and skill, then must leave the fruit of their efforts to someone who hasn't worked for it. This, too, is meaningless, a great tragedy. [22] So what do people get in this life for all their hard work and anxiety? [23] Their days of labor are filled with pain and grief; even at night their minds cannot rest. It is all meaningless. [24] So I decided there is nothing better than to enjoy food and drink and to find satisfaction in work. Then I realized that these pleasures are from the hand of God. [25] For who can eat or enjoy anything apart from him? [26] God gives wisdom, knowledge, and joy to those who please him. But if a sinner becomes wealthy, God takes the wealth away and gives it to those who please him. This, too, is meaningless—like chasing the wind.

{Ecclesiastes 3:1-22 NLT}-[1] For everything there is a season, a time for every activity under heaven. [2] A time to be born and a time to die. A time to plant and a time to harvest. [3] A time to kill and a time to heal. A time to tear down and a time to build up. [4] A time to cry and a time to laugh. A time to grieve and a time to dance. [5] A time to scatter stones and a time to gather stones. A time to embrace and a time to turn away. [6] A time to search and a time to quit searching. A time to keep and a time to throw away. [7] A time to tear and a time to mend. A time to be quiet and a time to speak. [8] A time to love and a time to hate. A time for war and a time for peace. [9] What do people really get for all their hard work? [10] I have seen the burden God has placed on us all. [11] Yet God has made everything beautiful for its own time. He has planted eternity in the human heart, but even so, people cannot see the whole scope of God's work from beginning to end. [12] So I concluded there is nothing better than to be happy and enjoy ourselves as long as we can. [13] And people should eat and drink and enjoy the fruits of their labor, for these are gifts from God. [14] And I know that whatever God does is final. Nothing can be added to it or taken from it. God's purpose is that people should fear him. [15] What is happening now has happened before, and what will happen in the future has happened before, because God makes the same things happen over and over again.

16] I also noticed that under the sun there is evil in the courtroom. Yes, even the courts of law are corrupt! [17] I said to myself, "In due season God will judge everyone, both good and bad, for all their deeds." [18] I also thought about the human condition—how God proves to people that they are like animals. [19] For people and animals share the same fate—both breathe and both must die. So people have no real advantage over the animals. How meaningless! [20] Both go to the same place—they came from dust and they return to dust. [21] For who can prove that the human spirit goes up and the spirit of animals goes down into the earth? [22] So I saw that there is nothing better for people than to be happy in their work. That is why we are here! No one will bring us back from death to enjoy life after we die.

{Ecclesiastes 4:1-16 NLT}-[1] Again, I observed all the oppression that takes place under the sun. I saw the tears of the oppressed, with no one to comfort them. The oppressors have great power, and their victims are helpless. [2] So I concluded that the dead are better off than the living.

[3] But most fortunate of all are those who are not yet born. For they have not seen all the evil that is done under the sun. [4] Then I observed that most people are motivated to success because they envy their neighbors. But this, too, is meaningless—like chasing the wind. [5] "Fools fold their idle hands, leading them to ruin." [6] And yet, "Better to have one handful with quietness than two handfuls with hard work and chasing the wind." [7] I observed yet another example of something meaningless under the sun. [8] This is the case of a man who is all alone, without a child or a brother, yet who works hard to gain as much wealth as he can. But then he asks

himself, "Who am I working for? Why am I giving up so much pleasure now?" It is all so meaningless and depressing. [9] Two people are better off than one, for they can help each other succeed. [10] If one person falls, the other can reach out and help. But someone who falls alone is in real trouble. [11] Likewise, two people lying close together can keep each other warm. But how can one be warm alone? [12] A person standing alone can be attacked and defeated, but two can stand back-to-back and conquer. Three are even better, for a triple-braided cord is not easily broken. [13] It is better to be a poor but wise youth than an old and foolish king who refuses all advice. [14] Such a youth could rise from poverty and succeed. He might even become king, though he has been in prison. [15] But then everyone rushes to the side of yet another youth who replaces him. [16] Endless crowds stand around him, but then another generation grows up and rejects him, too. So it is all meaningless—like chasing the wind.

{Ecclesiastes 5:1-20 NLT}-[1] As you enter the house of God, keep your ears open and your mouth shut. It is evil to make mindless offerings to God. [2] Don't make rash promises, and don't be hasty in bringing matters before God. After all, God is in heaven, and you are here on earth. So let your words be few. [3] Too much activity gives you restless dreams; too many words make you a fool. [4] When you make a promise to God, don't delay in following through, for God takes no pleasure in fools. Keep all the promises you make to him. [5] It is better to say nothing than to make a promise and not keep it. [6] Don't let your mouth make you sin. And don't defend yourself by telling the Temple messenger that the promise you made was a mistake. That would make God angry, and he might wipe out everything you have achieved. [7] Talk is cheap, like daydreams and other useless activities. Fear God instead. [8] Don't be surprised if you see a poor person being oppressed by the powerful and if justice is being miscarried throughout the land. For every official is under orders from higher up, and matters of justice get lost in red tape and bureaucracy. [9] Even the king milks the land for his own profit! [10] Those who love money will never have enough. How meaningless to think that wealth brings true happiness! [11] The more you have, the more people come to help you spend it. So what good is wealth—except perhaps to watch it slip through your fingers! [12] People who work hard sleep well, whether they eat little or much. But the rich seldom get a good night's sleep. [13] There is another serious problem I have seen under the sun. Hoarding riches harms the saver. [14] Money is put into risky investments that turn sour, and everything is lost. In the end, there is nothing left to pass on to one's children. [15] We all come to the end of our lives as naked and empty-handed as on the day we were born. We can't take our riches with us.

[16] And this, too, is a very serious problem. People leave this world no better off than when they came. All their hard work is for nothing—like working for the wind. [17] Throughout their lives, they live under a cloud—frustrated, discouraged, and angry. [18] Even so, I have noticed one thing, at least, that is good. It is good for people to eat, drink, and enjoy their work under the sun during the short life God has given them, and to accept their lot in life. [19] And it is a good thing to receive wealth from God and the good health to enjoy it. To enjoy your work and accept your lot in life—this is indeed a gift from God. [20] God keeps such people so busy enjoying life that they take no time to brood over the past.

CHAPTER 3

THE CROSS ROADS OF FAITH & BIBLE

{Jude 1:24-25 NKJV}-[24] Now to Him who is able to keep you from stumbling, And to present [you] faultless Before the presence of His glory with exceeding joy, [25] To God our Savior, Who alone is wise, [Be] glory and majesty, Dominion and power, Both now and forever. Amen.

We find cross roads in the Bible, through out the scriptures, but is the Bible fact or fiction? There are so many questions over the bible. So much controversy. The big questions ask most of the times are what is it, did God write it, Can I figure it out? The bible was meant to be understood by all believers who can read. Who takes serious interest in knowing the word of God! It is a complex piece of work. Hard to comprehend, but if you will stop relying on your own intellect, education and ask God for help, you will soon understand the word of God. Do not doubt the word of God in the Bible. However, by asking God you will have super-nature insight into the Bible. You must have the spirit of God to understand the Bible. The Bible is a message of salvation and a gift of God. The Bible is divine in origin and all the Bible is God-Breathed! Because they are, spirituality discerned the scoffers cannot understand the Bible it is foolishness to them.

We use the word canon when we talk about the Bible or describe it. The term canon is used in religion as being divinely inspired. Moreover, no God did not write the Bible, but He did inspire it. The entire Bible was God-Breath. The process of determining the canon was first conducted by Jewish rabbis and scholars and later by early Christians, ultimately it was God who decided what books are in the biblical canon.

The hard part in determining the biblical canon is that the Bible does not give a list of the books that belong in it. So some books are left out of it. By book, I mean writings and teachings and messengers sayings. It is importing to remember that a book or scripture belonged in the book the moment God had inspired the writing of it, again all of Gods inspired writings are not in the book, it was simply a matter for God which books should be included in the Bible.

The Bible has an old testament and a new testament. The Old Testament is before Jesus time, and the New Testament is from Jesus time on. The Old Testament is the Hebrew Bible. There was very little controversy over the canon of the Hebrew Old Testament, because the Hebrew believers recognized Gods messengers as from God. And they had first hand knowledge of the people who was writing it, and they accepted their writings as inspired by God. While there was undeniably debate over it, by AD 250 there was nearly universal agreement on it. Yet there is one issue that remained and that debate and discussion is continuing today.

The debate is over the Apocrypha writings as too are they divinely inspired. The majority of Hebrew scholars considered the Apocrypha writings to be good historical and religious documents, but not the same as Hebrew Scriptures. Now what are the Apocrypha scriptures? The term is usually applied to books that Hebrews and Christian considered useful but not divinely inspired and are excluded from the bible. For this reason, they are typically printing in a third section apart from the Bible. And in many editions, they are omitted entirely. The old testament Apocrypha consist of Jewish documents that were not accepted into the Hebrews Bible and the New Testament Apocrypha are those writings that were not accepted by ancient Christians.

The process of collection the New Testament scriptures begin in the first centuries of the Christian church, some of the books of the New Testament were circulated among the early churches at that time. The Muratorian Fragment is the oldest known list of New Testament books. And it was the first canon to be used. It was compiled in AD 170. It was discovered by Ludovic Antonion Muratori in the Ambrosian library in Milan. He published it in 1740; it is called a fragment because the list is missing the beginning. The fragment appears to have been copied in the 7th century. It is dated to about 170AD, because the author refers to Pius1 of Rome diocese. Pius1 was the ninth successor of Saint Peter and Saint Peter is credit with starting the Christian church. Pius1 jurisdiction was 2nd century Rome he rule the church in the middle 2nd century.

Church councils had influence over what books could be read in church. A church council is the highest from of ecclesiastical authority. Now they would assembly church officials and theologians for matters of doctrine and conduct etc. I just name a couple of them that had something to say about the

Bible; these are not the only ones. In AD 363, the council of Laodicea said that the Old Testament along with 27 books of the New Testament was to be read in the churches. The council took place soon after the war between the Rome Empire and the Persians. The council had concerns over the conduct of church members so they made a decree about what books are to be read.

The council of Hippo AD 393 and the council of Carthage AD 397 affirmed the same 27 books of the New Testament. This council determine whether or not a book was truly inspired by God. It is crucial to remember that the council did not determine the canon; it was God alone who pick which books belonged in the Bible.

The human process of collecting the books was flawed, but it was God who brought the church to see that it was He who had inspired the books. Yes, it is truly Gods word. The fact that God gave us the Bible is evidence of his love for us. And that He communicated to us what He is like and how we can have a relationship with Him are things we would not have known.

The question we ask is how can we know that the Bible is the word of God? And not just a good book? There is no doubt that the Bible does claim to be the word of God. Paul said to Timothy you have known the Holy Scriptures, which makes you wise in salvation through faith in Jesus, All scriptures that is God-Breathed.

All Scripture is given by inspiration of God, and is profitable for doctrine, for reproof, for correction, for instruction in righteousness, The Bible is 66 individual books, written over 3 centuries, in three languages at the time, and over approximately 1500 years, and by more than 40 authors, yet it remains unified from beginning to end. This is more evidence that God gave us his words to record.

Archeologists continue to find and unearth evidence of ancient people and cultures all described in the Bible. The descriptions of these ancient cultures have proven to be completely reliable and accurate. The Bible is prophetic and 30% of it actually contains scriptures predicting future events. Bible prophecies are extremely detailed. Over 1800 prophecies that foretell specific details about the messiah, Israel and other nations have come true not just true but 100% accurate.

The Bible is honest, look at how painfully honest it is. Jacob one of the fathers of the Jew says he was a deceiver, Moses the law giver was a murderer, king David one of Israel's beloved an adulterer, Paul wrote over ½ of the new testament was once one of the worst of sinners.

Christians have a near consensus on what the Bible says, but have different methods of interpreting the text. As a result, they reach different conclusions about what a passage actually means. Some use Hermeneutic method of interpreting. This is the art and science of interpreting written texts. To do this you use the proper application of the language and proper historical setting, thoughts and attitudes at the time of writing and more. To use Hermeneutic to interpret is way too much for me, I let the word of God speak for it self.

I do use Dr. D. L. Cooper rule of interpretation. (When the plain sense of Scripture makes common sense, seek no other sense) We are to assume the bible means exactly what it says. Examples of passages that are not intended to be taken literally are parables, dreams, visions these are symbolically. Remember that they do stand for something and have a literal meaning. You must find the literal meaning behind it.

The modern Bible is divided by chapter and verse and books and old & New Testament.

Examples are John 5:3-7 book of John is in the New Testament chapter 5, verses 3 through 7 or

Jo. 5:3-7 {NLT} book of John chapter 5 Verses 3 through 7 New Living Translation. (version)

There are a number of different versions of the Bible, but there is eight primary versions. Found in history 1 Septuagint 250 AD in Greek, 2 Vulgate 400 AD in Latin, 3Luther 1534AD German, 4 King James 1611AD but has a large number of errors because none of the writers had a decent amount of understanding of Hebrew, 5 Revised standard version 1952AD American English, 6 New International version 1960AD good contemporary English, 7 The Young's Literal Translation as close to the originals of the Hebrew and Greek was translated 1898AD, 8 New Living Translation To convey the meaning of the ancient Hebrew and Greek texts to modern reader.

The Bible is God's source and power for faith. The gospel of Jesus Christ is God's plain for our salvation through faith. It shows how through faith we can be saved. It is imperative that we come to faith. We are in the season. That great and terrible day will be here soon, too soon for some and not soon enough for others. Which do you want to be like? We are that generation we are seeing the events and turning points that Jesus was talking about each and every day now. We are seeing more and more of these signs. No other pursuit is as urgent as the quest for faith, and we must understand exactly what it is, and how we can have it. What does the Bible have to say about faith? I have found no definition of faith in the Bible. When you look up the word faith, it occurs 250 times in 232 verses in the {NASB} and 235 times in 212 verses in the {NLT} versions of the bible. The word faith seems to describe what faith can do, than what it is.

Jesus Christ is about break out into the open with his rule and set up his kingdom for 1000 years. We can all be saved no matter what we have done. We are made right in God's sight when we believe his promise to take away our sins. All we have to do is trust in Jesus Christ and call on his name. For all have sinned and are falling short of God's standard. There is only one path that leads to God. There is only one God, and there is only one way of being accepted. And that way makes our sins go away by faith in Jesus Christ You do receive God's approval because of your faith, but faith is like riding a bike first you must acquire some skill. You do fall a few times, so to you can fall from your faith but like that bike, you climb back on it. You had faith that you could ride that bike. So have faith in faith and remember the skills you have acquire and repent and ask God to forgive you. We all must go through many tribulations.

In Luke 22, Jesus said Simon, Satan has asked to have all of you, to sift you like wheat. (Webster's dictionary of sift, separate, examine with close scrutiny.) The devil had desire to examine all of Simon faith, he wanted to separate him from the faith that he had. Simon did not lose his faith, he just fell off that bike. His faith was thin or weak and he was not convinced of his faith. He had little confidence and he was a backslider. Simon did get back on that bike (faith) through repenting and he return to his faith even stronger than before.

Faith is not a think that you buy like a piece of furniture, or is it an attitude you cultivate through positive thinking. Although it does work, but only to the degree you can conjure it up. Faith is believing in what God has promised, where positive thinking is something you do on your own merit. Positive thinking is very useful or even necessary in achieving faith, but not on your merit, you must ask God to help you. We can use positive thinking to gather our thoughts, but the LORD gives the right answer. You must commit your thoughts to the LORD, and then your plans will succeed.

Faith is not just positive thinking or will power; you do not just conjure it up. Faith is a free gift from God, a perfect gift. With all gifts from God, you must ask for it. The light bulb makes no effort to come on until you hit the switch. Wishing for it will not work, you must ask. Did you wish you could ride that bike, no you had to climb on it and acquire some skill, oh you might have wish you could ride the bike but you had to get on it first. Faith is a day-by-day situation that we must face. Life is of course full of problems, involving temptation, trails, suffering, forgiveness and more. Faith does not give any guarantees to an easy life, but it does guarantee an eternity. Faith will begin for most of us in very small quantity.

The mustard seed is the smallest of seeds, but can grow to be a tree. It will not grow until it is planted and the ground receives it, without nourishment it will not grow. This is faith, you must look for it and you must receive it, and you must give it nourishment. Like yeast, it will only take a little bit to permeated through you.

Try exposing yourself to religion, it can be contagious. Try reading the Bible; you will not catch faith if you do not give it a try. You will not be able to catch it buy staying away from church, or the Bible. Sitting in a church and going to places to hear about God isn't enough either. It is essential that you ask God for faith, and to believe in faith and in that way you will catch it. If you think that you cannot catch faith or that you could never have real faith, all you have to do is just ask God. If you think that you cannot have faith like this, it would be like twisting off the tap to the shut off the water and looking for the water to come on. You would be shutting yourself off from God and his will for you. God will help if you really search for him, and are honest about yourself, and you hope and pray for faith.

I suggest you try taking a long hard look at yourself, and be honest. Look to see if there is anything holding you back, anger, hatred, jealousy, resentment, fear, and guilt are just some of the ways the devil will use to get in your way of faith. It is important to surrender these faults to God. If you make a sincere effort, you will find that a little faith will go a long way. You will not get ride of sin unless you get ride of your ways. This is what Jesus meant by being born again. You can have a new life and new goals with faith. You will be transformed into someone of faith and be born again.

The lord protects those of child like faith, the child does not use principles of reasoning all the reasoning they need is what they where told. The child will accept without any proof or evidence what the Father or Mother say, they have trust in what the parents say. You will need to have faith like that child, faith in the Father in heaven and your faith is far more precious to God the father than mere gold. If your faith remains strong after all the trails we must go through, it will bring you much praise and glory and honor on the day when Jesus Christ is revealed to the whole world. Your reward for trusting him with child like faith will be the salvation of your soul.

In Psalms 116:6 it says a none believer a sinner facing death. Jesus saved him because he became a believer with child like faith. He was bore again and transformed into someone of faith. We all face death that do evil, sin, and then do not repent. If a evil sinner will repent, they may face physical death but not spiritual death (the soul). And do not fear those who kill the body but cannot kill the soul; rather fear him who can destroy both soul and body in hell.

As you know Satan, the devil knows prophecy? That's why he parallels everything in the bible and he uses that to confuse you. That's why we have so many false religions, it so Satan can deny the truth that the trinity of God is the Father and Son and Holy Spirit, and that Jesus came in the flesh to save the world. You should not believe every spirit, but test the spirits, whether they are of God. You will know the Spirit is from God if that spirit confesses that Jesus Christ has come in the flesh is of God, Every spirit from God will say Jesus is the son of God and he came in the flesh.

The spirit of God teaches us what the truth is. The Holy Spirit lives in all who knows the truth. The Holy Spirit is the truth and teaches all things. Anyone who denies the Son doesn't have the Father, but all who confesses the Son has the Father. The Good News is at work to make all right in God's sight. This is accomplished by faith. The scriptures say, "it is through faith that a righteous person has life" Faith in Jesus Christ as the Son of God and that God raised him from the dead. God does show his anger from heaven against all sinful, wicked people who push the truth away from themselves.

The scriptures also say that since the creation of the world, we have been able to see the power and divine nature and invisible attributes that are God's, we have seen clearly and understood from what he made so we have no excuse to not know the truth about God. For God is known to us instinctively, God put this knowledge in our hearts. All sinful wicked people can clearly see God's invisible qualities and his eternal power and his divine nature. We have no excuse what so ever for not knowing God.

Now those of you, who think that they live by the law and do right, but do not know the truth, are not saved. God put the same knowledge in you, so when you refuse to understand the truth God will abandon you just as he does to all sinful wicked people. You and they refuse to understand the truth. The death penalty is for all who refuse to confess the truth, no mater how good of a person they may be.

The scriptures tell us that Abraham the founder of the Jewish nation, that he believed in God, and it was his faith in God that God declared him to be righteous. It was Abraham faith that brought him into a relationship with God. So if you think and declare that you are good enough to be saved, then what you are saying is that faith is useless and in that case God's promises are also useless and meaningless. Nevertheless, by now you should know that faith is the key too God's promises. God's promises are a free gift to those who have faith, and for those who ask God for faith. You are certain to receive them if you have the kind of faith that Abraham had. The scriptures say Abraham is the Father of all who believe.

{Galatians 3:1-29 NLT}-[1] Oh, foolish Galatians! Who has cast an evil spell on you? For the meaning of Jesus Christ's death was made as clear to you as if you had seen a picture of his death on the cross. [2]

Let me ask you this one question: Did you receive the Holy Spirit by obeying the law of Moses? Of course not! You received the Spirit because you believed the message you heard about Christ. [3] How foolish can you be? After starting your Christian lives in the Spirit, why are you now trying to become perfect by your own human effort? [4] Have you experienced so much for nothing? Surely it was not in vain, was it? [5] I ask you again, does God give you the Holy Spirit and work miracles among you because you obey the law? Of course not! It is because you believe the message you heard about Christ. [6] In the same way, "Abraham believed God, and God counted him as righteous because of his faith." [7] The real children of Abraham, then, are those who put their faith in God. [8] What's more, the Scriptures looked forward to this time when God would declare the Gentiles to be righteous because of their faith. God proclaimed this good news to Abraham long ago when he said, "All nations will be blessed through you." [9] So all who put their faith in Christ share the same blessing Abraham received because of his faith. [10] But those who depend on the law to make them right with God are under his curse, for the Scriptures say, "Cursed is everyone who does not observe and obey all the commands that are written in God's Book of the Law." [11] So it is clear that no one can be made right with God by trying to keep the law. For the Scriptures say,

"It is through faith that a righteous person has life." [12] This way of faith is very different from the way of law, which says, "It is through obeying the law that a person has life." [13] But Christ has rescued us from the curse pronounced by the law. When he was hung on the cross, he took upon himself the curse for our wrongdoing. For it is written in the Scriptures, "Cursed is everyone who is hung on a tree."

[14] Through Christ Jesus, God has blessed the Gentiles with the same blessing he promised to Abraham, so that we who are believers might receive the promised Holy Spirit through faith. [15] Dear brothers and sisters, here's an example from everyday life. Just as no one can set aside or amend an irrevocable agreement, so it is in this case. [16] God gave the promises to Abraham and his child. And notice that the Scripture doesn't say "to his children," as if it meant many descendants. Rather, it says "to his child"—and that, of course, means Christ. [17] This is what I am trying to say: The agreement God made with Abraham could not be canceled 430 years later when God gave the law to Moses. God would be breaking his promise. [18] For if the inheritance could be received by keeping the law, then it would not be the result of accepting God's promise. But God graciously gave it to Abraham as a promise. [19] Why, then, was the law given? It was given alongside the promise to show people their sins. But the law was

designed to last only until the coming of the child who was promised. God gave his law through angels to Moses, who was the mediator between God and the people. [20] Now a mediator is helpful if more than one party must reach an agreement. But God, who is one, did not use a mediator when he gave his promise to Abraham. [21] Is there a conflict, then, between God's law and God's promises? Absolutely not! If the law could give us new life, we could be made right with God by obeying it. [22] But the Scriptures declare that we are all prisoners of sin, so we receive God's promise of freedom only by believing in Jesus Christ. [23] Before the way of faith in Christ was available to us, we were placed under guard by the law. We were kept in protective custody, so to speak, until the way of faith was revealed. [24] Let me put it another way. The law was our guardian until Christ came; it protected us until we could be made right with God through faith. [25] And now that the way of faith has come, we no longer need the law as our guardian. [26] For you are all children of God through faith in Christ Jesus. [27] And all who have been united with Christ in baptism have put on Christ, like putting on new clothes. [28] There is no longer Jew or Gentile, slave or free, male and female. For you are all one in Christ Jesus. [29] And now that you belong to Christ, you are the true children of Abraham. You are his heirs, and God's promise to Abraham belongs to you.

{Galatians 4:1-31 NLT}-[1] Think of it this way. If a father dies and leaves an inheritance for his young children, those children are not much better off than slaves until they grow up, even though they actually own everything their father had. [2] They have to obey their guardians until they reach whatever age their father set. [3] And that's the way it was with us before Christ came. We were like children; we were slaves to the basic spiritual principles of this world. [4] But when the right time came, God sent his Son, born of a woman, subject to the law. [5] God sent him to buy freedom for us who were slaves to the law, so that he could adopt us as his very own children

. [6] And because we are his children, God has sent the Spirit of his Son into our hearts, prompting us to call out, "Abba, Father."

[7] Now you are no longer a slave but God's own child. And since you are his child, God has made you his heir. [8] Before you Gentiles knew God, you were slaves to so-called gods that do not even exist. [9] So now that you know God (or should I say, now that God knows you), why do you want to go back again and become slaves once more to the weak and useless spiritual principles of this world? [10] You are trying to earn favor with God by observing certain days or months or seasons or years. [11] I fear for you. Perhaps all my hard work with you was for nothing.

[12] Dear brothers and sisters, I plead with you to live as I do in freedom from these things, for I have become like you Gentiles—free from those laws. You did not mistreat me when I first preached to you. [13] Surely you remember that I was sick when I first brought you the Good News. [14] But even though my condition tempted you to reject me, you did not despise me or turn me away. No, you took me in and cared for me as though I were an angel from God or even Christ Jesus himself. [15] Where is that joyful and grateful spirit you felt then? I am sure you would have taken out your own eyes and given them to me if it had been possible. [16] Have I now become your enemy because I am telling you the truth? [17] Those false teachers are so eager to win your favor, but their intentions are not good. They are trying to shut you off from me so that you will pay attention only to them. [18] If someone is eager to do good things for you, that's all right; but let them do it all the time, not just when I'm with you. [19] Oh, my dear children! I feel as if I'm going through labor pains for you again, and they will continue until Christ is fully developed in your lives. [20] I wish I were with you right now so I could change my tone. But at this distance I don't know how else to help you. [21] Tell me, you who want to live under the law, do you know what the law actually says? [22] The Scriptures say that Abraham had two sons, one from his slave

wife and one from his freeborn wife. [23] The son of the slave wife was born in a human attempt to bring about the fulfillment of God's promise. But the son of the freeborn wife was born as God's own fulfillment of his promise. [24] These two women serve as an illustration of God's two covenants. The first woman, Hagar, represents Mount Sinai where people received the law that enslaved them. [25] And now Jerusalem is just like Mount Sinai in Arabia, because she and her children live in slavery to the law. [26] But the other woman, Sarah, represents the heavenly Jerusalem. She is the free woman, and she is our mother. [27] As Isaiah said, "Rejoice, O childless woman, you who have never given birth! Break into a joyful shout, you who have never been in labor! For the desolate woman now has more children than the woman who lives with her husband!" [28] And you, dear brothers and sisters, are children of the promise, just like Isaac. [29] But you are now being persecuted by those who want you to keep the law, just as Ishmael, the child born by human effort, persecuted Isaac, the child born by the power of the Spirit. [30] But what do the Scriptures say about that? "Get rid of the slave and her son, for the son of the slave woman will not share the inheritance with the free woman's son." [31] So, dear brothers and sisters, we are not children of the slave woman; we are children of the free woman.

CHAPTER 4

THE TURNING POINTS OF THE RAPTURE

The event we call the rapture, is used as caught up in the Bible, caught up in the clouds to meet the Lord in the air. The rapture the sudden vanishing of millions of Christians from all over the world will vanish without a trace. The Bible tells us the reason for the mass disappearance. The church is not destined for the wrath of God. The Bible does warn believers to be ready and looking for the blessed hope. The word rapture does not appear in the English translations, but in the Latin Vulgate a version of the Bible authorized and used by the Roman Catholic Church, the word Rapiemur is used, and this is where I think the word rapture comes from.

The rapture is a means of escape for the church, which is made up of all Christians who believe in Jesus Christ, who are living or who have died believing in the truth. Escape from the tribulation, Jesus will come and get them so they can escape the wrath of God. The tribulation is a time of testing for those who dwell on the face of the earth after the rapture, those who will be left will not be believers. All believers are to be on alert at all times, praying to escape all these things that are coming to the earth. They are to be looking for the blessed hope, the appearing of the savior.

In Luke 21 it says that when we see these things (turning points) begin to happen look up, your salvation is near. Your salvation is in the blessed hope; the blessed hope is the appearing of Jesus Christ. We cannot imagine what we will become like when Jesus returns, but we do know we will be like him and we will see him as he relay is. God will give all Christians glorious resurrection bodies for eternity. Our earthly bodies, which die, will be different when they are resurrected and never die. The new bodies will be suitable for an eternity. We will be transformed just as the scriptures say we will.

Christians are looking for the appearance of Jesus and not the return. Because when he returns, he will be bringing all of them with him. Because when the rapture does come he will appear in the air and not return yet. This is the blessed hope. God has not destined the church for the wrath. God has revealed a secret; not all will die but will be transformed in the twinkling of an eye. It will happen in a moment, the Christians who have died will be resurrected with transformed bodies, and then those who are living will receive there transformed bodies and never die.

The scripture tells us everyone dies because all are related to Adam, the first man. However, all who are related to Christ, those who believe in him will be given a new life, by Jesus the other man who was resurrected. Nevertheless, because of the rapture the Christians who are living will never die but are transformed to immortality. However, there is an order to the resurrection; Jesus Christ was raised first, and now all Christians who believe in the truth will be raised, the truth that Jesus paid the price for our sins.

Are you ready for the rapture? The only requirement is to be born again by accepting Jesus Christ as your Lord and savior. Jesus promised that if we repent of our sins, and confess him Lord and savior we would have eternal life. If you are not ready for the rapture now is the time, you should get rid of any questions you might have about your salvation, and get ready to meet Jesus in the sky when he comes for his bride the church. God will leave everyone who is not saved on the earth, when the rapture occurs, they will have to go through the tribulation, the time of God's wrath.

The day is coming when he returns for his bride the church, unless you have a death wish or would like to go through the tribulation. You will surely want to go with the church at the time of the rapture. The only way is to accept Jesus atonement for your sins. By accept his payment, for our sin debt to God, this includes believing in his death, burial and resurrection and to repent of sins and confess him Lord and saver.

Are you ready for it? If not, tomorrow could literally be too late. So make you decision today for Jesus Christ. Every person's destiny of eternal life is whether they accepted Jesus Christ payment for there sins. Rapture or tribulation this is the choice you make when you accept the pardon for sin as provided by Jesus. Do you choose the truth so you will be saved, or do you chose to remain in an unrepentant state, and if you are alive at the time, you will have to go through the wrath of God. So make your decision now, so if the rapture comes right now you will be saved. Make you decision now because you do not want die in sin and not be saved. So when Jesus does come you will be resurrected to an eternal life. The Bible says that the gate is narrow that leads to salvation, and wide is the gate to hell! Rapture or tribulation is yours to choose. Since the fall of man in the Garden of Eden, man has been under a terrible curse, but God has provided for us a remedy for this curse. That remedy is the blood of Jesus Christ that he shed on the cross and paid that sin debt in full.

In Matthew ((22:2-14) NLT Bible-the kingdom of Heaven is illustrated by the story of a king who prepared a great wedding feast for his son.

{Matthew 22:1-14 NKJV}-[1] And Jesus answered and spoke to them again by parables and said: [2] "The kingdom of heaven is like a certain king who arranged a marriage for his son, [3] "and sent out his servants to call those who were invited to the wedding; and they were not willing to come. [4] "Again, he sent out other servants, saying, 'Tell those who are invited, "See, I have prepared my dinner; my oxen and fatted cattle [are] killed, and all things [are] ready. Come to the wedding." '[5] "But they made light of it and went their ways, one to his own farm, and another to his business. [6] "And the rest seized his servants, treated [them] spitefully, and killed [them].

[7] "But when the king heard [about it], he was furious. And he sent out his armies, destroyed those murderers, and burned up their city. [8] "Then he said to his servants, 'The wedding is ready, but those who were invited were not worthy.[9] 'Therefore go into the highways, and as many as you find, invite to the wedding.' [10] "So those servants went out into

the highways and gathered together all whom they found, both bad and good. And the wedding [hall] was filled with guests. [11] "But when the king came in to see the guests, he saw a man there who did not have on a wedding garment. [12] "So he said to him, 'Friend, how did you come in here without a wedding garment?' And he was speechless. [13] "Then the king said to the servants, 'Bind him hand and foot, take him away, and cast [him] into outer darkness; there will be weeping and gnashing of teeth.' [14] "For many are called, but few [are] chosen."

The king is God the Father and the son is Jesus Christ and the wedding feast is the Lamb (Jesus) to the bride (the church). When the banquet was ready the invited guest was the Jews, and the banquet that was ready was the first time Jesus came, but they refused to believed in the truth. The servants that were killed for telling the guest to come was Jesus Christ disciples. So God had punish the invited guest the Jew. So he invited all to come gentile and pagan, the good and bad this is how all can come to Christ. The man not in wedding clothes is anyone who does not believe the truth, on judgment day God will throw them out of his sight. Many hear the world but do not understand, many know of Jesus but few choose to believe the truth. The scripture in Revelation below shows us that there is a wedding feast, and how we should be glade.

{Revelation 19:7-8 NKJV}-[7] "Let us be glad and rejoice and give Him glory, for the marriage of the Lamb has come, and His wife has made herself ready." [8] And to her it was granted to be arrayed in fine linen, clean and bright, for the fine linen is the righteous acts of the saints.

A question that gets ask a lot is does the turning point of the rapture mark the beginning of the tribulation? The Bible does not state anywhere that the tribulation begins with the rapture. The rapture could occur at anytime, although it is likely to occur near the beginning because the tribulation is the time of God's wrath. And those who go in the rapture are not destined to go through the tribulation. Probable the two most controversial topic in the Bible are the rapture and the tribulation periods. It has to do with the timing of these events. Is the rapture per-tribulation, mid-tribulation, post-tribulation? What we must remember is that the tribulation is center around the antichrist, the mark of the beast and the number 666, and around the false prophet and that the Church is not destined for God's wrath and much more. Therefore, this is why I take the per-tribulation point of view, but no matter what point of view you do take, all that you really need to know is that all this is going to happen and happen very soon.

{1 Thessalonians 5:9-10 NLT}-[9] For God chose to save us through our Lord Jesus Christ, not to pour out his anger on us. [10] Christ died for us so that, whether we are dead or alive when he returns, we can live with him forever.

The scriptures say that the man of lawlessness cannot be revealed until what is holding him back is taken out of the way. The restrainer is the Holy Spirit, and the Holy Spirit reside in all believers, Christians who are the church, thus, when the church is removed (Christians) the antichrist will be unleashed on the world, and the tribulation can begin. The prophet Daniel said a covenant for seven years between the antichrist and Israel for peace would come is the starting point of the tribulation, and this is so the Jews can rebuild their temple In addition, the book off revelation implies per-tribulation rapture without mentioning the event as the rapture. In Revelation 19 John sees the heavens open and Jesus comes on a white horse and the believers coming with him, the believers are the church, so if they are coming with him, then they must have been rapture.

{2 Thessalonians 2:1-7 NKJV}-[1] Now, brethren, concerning the coming of our Lord Jesus Christ and our gathering together to Him, we ask you, [2] not to be soon shaken in mind or troubled, either by spirit or by word or by letter, as if from us, as though the day of Christ had come. [3] Let no one deceive you by any means; for [that Day will not come] unless the falling away comes first, and the man of sin is revealed, the son of perdition, [4] who opposes and exalts himself above all that is called God or that is worshiped, so that he sits as God in the temple of God, showing himself that he is God. [5] Do you not remember that when I was still with you I told you these things? [6] And now you know what is restraining, that he may be revealed in his own time. [7] For the mystery of lawlessness is already at work; only He who now restrains [will do so] until He is taken out of the way.

In Luke 21 its says when all these things being to happen, to look up, note that our salvation will come when these signs begins. The rapture is a secret event and can happen anytime. The sings or turning points are all around us for the tribulation period to began, more, more are coming quickly each day, and we see turning points everywhere. Therefore, you can figure out that the rapture is ever so close as well.

CHAPTER 5

THE TURNING POINTS OF REVELATION

It is believed that the apostle John wrote the book of Revelation while in exile on the island of Patmos, off the coast of present day turkey. Revelation was probably written around A.D. 95-96. The book is probably the most symbolic language in the bible. It was addressed to seven actual church that existed at that time. Revelation begins with letters to these churches from Jesus Christ himself. These letters include commendations, criticism, and comfort.

After the letters comes highly symbolic language, that covers visions of judgment on the wicked. John described visions given to him by God, about the rapture, tribulation, the antichrist and the false prophet, Armageddon, mark of the beast and the second coming of Jesus Christ and more.

It was around A.D. 95-96, over 60+ years that Jesus walk the earth. Of all the disciples John was the only one still alive. John had written his gospel of Jesus Christ 25 years earlier and around 15 years later he wrote his three letters. He was for a time the Bishop of the church in Ephesus, he and the mother of our Lord, Mary moved there in about 70 A.D.

The Romans with the help of the Jews had beheaded Paul and had crucified Peter in Rome around 65 A.D. They'd tried several times to kill John but had no luck. One time they put him in boiling oil, but like all the other time the Lord prevented it from harming him. Finally the Romans had him exiled to a prison colony off the coast of Modern day Turkey, the Island of Patmos. I am sure the Romans were thinking that's the last time we will hear anything from him. However, God had other plans for him. John was about to undertake one of his greatest challenges, the writing of the book of Revelation at the end of his life as an old man.

The Lord appeared personally to John commanding him to write one final letter, (the book of Revelation) and to send it to the seven churches in Asia Minor. After writing the book he died of natural causes in about A.D.100. The book of revelation can be hard to understand at first look. Don't be foolish to thing it is apocalyptic and you will never understand it. Although it is prophetic literature that does use a lot of symbols, a sort of Alice and wonderland story. With practice and some help from some good books you will began to see it all come together.

The symbols do stand for something. They have a literal meaning. They were not just willy-nilly selected by God. You must look for the literal meaning behind it. God doesn't write in riddles to purposefully confuse us. He says what he means and means what he says. You should try always to accept the plain sense meaning, put aside what is confusing and hang on to what you understand, and come back to what you are confuse on later on.

Accepting the plain sense meaning applies when you don't understand the passage. Think of this as an example in {*Revelation 9:16 NLT*}-*[16] I heard the size of their army, which was 200 million mounted troops.*

At the time of the writing of this there weren't even 200 million people in the world. Can you imagine the early readers trying to figure it out? To day one nation has 200 million in their arms, China can send an army that large.

Dr. Cyrus Ingerson Scofield (1843-1921) is known for the Scofield reference bible. He produced the study bible with explanatory notes. He gave literal interpretation of passage; the very first was in 1909. He had concluding in Ezekiel 38-39 that Russia and her allies will invade Israel in the end times most scholars still accept this literal meaning today. However, in 1909 Israel did not exist nor was there any prospect that it every would. Commenting on it he stated" I don't understand it, and I can't explain it. But that is what it says. Therefore, I believe it."

In {Revelation 13:15 NLT} the scriptures say the false prophet was permitted to let the image speak. For many of years people had to wonder how you could make a image speak, a many scholars wrote all kinds of spirituality explanations. But today you can see how with all the modern technology it could speak. When the Bible says the false prophet will make an image speak, I thing we should believe the Bible means what it says. By accepting the plain sense, you will know when it does not make plain sense.

{Revelation 13:15-17 NKJV}-[15] He was granted [power] to give breath to the image of the beast, that the image of the beast should both speak and cause as many as would not worship the image of the beast to be killed. [16] He causes all, both small and great, rich and poor, free and slave, to receive a mark on their right hand or on their foreheads, [17] and that no one may buy or sell except one who has the mark or the name of the beast, or the number of his name.

The kind of technology we have with computers today a mark such as this is possible. The early readers had to accept this by the plain sense that the passage meant what it said. You will start to understand the book of Revelation if you accept the plain sense of it, and believe that symbols stand for something literal.

Remember there are many books out there to help you with Revelation. But accept the plain sense of these books. Remember Dr. D. L. Cooper rule of interpretation "when the plain sense of scriptures makes common sense seek no other sense." Let me say here the book of revelation is prophecy and that prophecy has an order to it. But the book was written in the order in which the truth was revealed to John, but the events described are not necessarily in chronological order. But the seven letters are in order. The rest of the book has a lot do with the tribulation and the wrath of God. God's wrath will consist of events that are called judgments. There are three sets of seven, making 21 judgments that consist of the wrath of God. There are 7-sealed scroll, 7 trumpet and 7 bowl judgments.

John was writing to the seven churches of Asia Minor, but consensus is that these churches seem to representative all churches in every generation, throughout the church age, and represent varying spiritual conditions of all the churches throughout history. Each message is also addressed to individuals to show the kind of spiritual fight that they can encounter. Also you see the promises are given to those who overcomes, and he who hears. One more theory is that the seven churches represent seven periods of the church age throughout history, with the church of Laodicea as the final church at the time of Jesus Christ coming. I believe and accept all of the above. We are in the age of the church of Laodicea, you can see it every day how Christian are lukewarm for God the Father and the son Jesus Christ. They don't have time for God or Jesus, there are neither hot nor cold for the truth.

At the end of the letters to the churches, God gives a invitation to those who listen and come to Jesus Christ.

Revelation 3:20-22 NKJV}-[20] "Behold, I stand at the door and knock. If anyone hears My voice and opens the door, I will come in to him and dine with him, and he with Me. [21] "To him who overcomes

I will grant to sit with Me on My throne, as I also overcame and sat down with My Father on His throne. [22] "He who has an ear, let him hear what the Spirit says to the churches."

The invitation Jesus extends here extends to those who wish to come to God the Father. Is a most gracious gift and illustrates that God is always available to those who are willing to put their trust in Jesus and come to God. Where God says, "He who has an ear, let him hear what the spirit says to the churches.", depends on individuals hearing and doing what they hear, they must respond to the word of God.

The worst part is in so many cases no one is listening. They are neither hot nor cold for the word of God. What is cover in the book of revaluation is the tribulation, and wars,famine,plagues,natural disaster,antichrist,the beast the abomination of desolation, covenant for peace, temple to be rebuild for the Jew's and much much more. However, to go over all this it would take a book all on its own.

{Revelation 19:11-14 NKJV}-[11] Now I saw heaven opened, and behold, a white horse. And He who sat on him [was] called Faithful and True, and in righteousness He judges and makes war. [12] His eyes [were] like a flame of fire, and on His head [were] many crowns. He had a name written that no one knew except Himself. [13] He [was] clothed with a robe dipped in blood, and His name is called The Word of God. [14] And the armies in heaven, clothed in fine linen, white and clean, followed Him on white horses.

CHAPTER 6

THE TURNING POINTS OF THE TRIBULATION

{Matthew 24:21-22, 25 NKJV}-[21] "For then there will be great tribulation, such as has not been since the beginning of the world until this time, no, nor ever shall be. [22] "And unless those days were shortened, no flesh would be saved; but for the elect's sake those days will be shortened…[25] "See, I have told you beforehand.

The tribulation is that time God, will pour out his wrath upon the inhabitants of the earth, and by now you know very will that the inhabitants of the earth is those who God will leave on the earth, who are not saved when the rapture occurs. That great and terrible time of the tribulation is coming, it will be far worse than any biblical plagues so far. That great and terrible time is a time for judgment, the 21 judgments of the tribulation. The horror of the tribulation is so terrible that Jesus said if it was not stopped; it would result in no life at all. In the book of revaluation, the apostle John states of that time, the tribulation would be so great that the leaders of the world would try to hid in caves and cry out for the rocks and mountains to fall on them. This tribulation is for seven years, the 21 judgments will be in two parts three-and-a-half years each.

The Bible distinguishes between the first half of the tribulation and the final three-and-a-half years. When the tribulation begins this will be only the beginning of the horrors to come. The final three-and-a-half years are known as the Great Tribulation. It will begin with the abomination of desolation and end with the return of Jesus Christ. This person the Antichrist will break the covenant with the Jews and persecution will increase on the Jews and anyone who believes in God the Father of Jesus Christ. This is the time of the war in heaven, Revelation 12:7. (The final three-and-a-half years).

{Revelation 12:7-10, 12 NKJV}-[7] And war broke out in heaven: Michael and his angels fought with the dragon; and the dragon and his angels fought, [8] but they did not prevail, nor was a place found for them in heaven any longer. [9] So the great dragon was cast out, that serpent of old, called the Devil and Satan, who deceives the whole world; he was cast to the earth, and his angels were cast out with him. [10] Then I heard a loud voice saying in heaven, "Now salvation, and strength, and the kingdom of our God, and the power of His Christ have come, for the accuser of our brethren, who accused them before our God day and night, has been cast down...

[12] "Therefore rejoice, O heavens, and you who dwell in them! Woe to the inhabitants of the earth and the sea! For the devil has come down to you, having great wrath, because he knows that he has a short time."

You ask, how can a God of love and grace and mercy allow such terror and bloodshed? He is a God of perfect justice, and he must deal with sin. His justice demands it. He will not over look sin. The Lord is slow to anger; he has allow man to sin over long periods of time. Because he does not want any to perish, instead he wants all to come to repentance. But there is a day that his is going to judge all sin. Amazingly, the tribulation is to bring people salvation. God's purpose is to save all, but he must destroy those who do not want salvation. You see when the earth goes through the tribulation and judgments the inhabitants of the earth learn righteousness. The truth is God will use the tribulation to get the attention of sinners and to motivate them to repentance. The strange truth is most people will respond to such discipline as to continually to ignore him, or will be cursing God for doing so.

Babylon one of the worlds magnificent Empires throughout human history had conquered most of the known world and brought untold numbers of slaves back to Babylon. Among the slaves was a young Hebrew prophets name Daniel, who had become one of the greatest person to see future turning points. God gave Daniel visions of the future and the ability to interpret dreams. Daniel saw the unfolding of many turning points of human history, giving us a highly detailed look into our future, and the time Jesus Christ was on the earth, he had visions describing the end of days—the time that we are now in or about to enter.

The prophecy of Daniel tells us exactly what will start the seven years of the tribulation. The Antichrist will make a covenant with the nation Israel for seven years, that covenant will be in a form of a peace treaty. The events of the tribulation will follow the rapture of the church. Their could be a preparation time period be twine the rapture and the tribulation. This preparation time is used to set up for the tribulation, because there is going to be a ten-nation group forming a Middle East political group. A leader will emerge (Antichrist) who will gain control over three of the ten nations and then over all ten nation. He will need this political position of power in the Middle East to enter into a covenant of peace with Israel. This covenant will start the seven-years of the tribulation.

The first half of the seven years will be a time of peace as the covenant is observed. However, the tribulation judgments on the world are still going on. In the middle of the seven years, the peace treaty will be broken by the Antichrist. The Antichrist will proclaim to be ruler over the entire earth. He will set up a one-world government empire In Babylon. The end of his reign is the world war we call Armageddon, this is where Babylon will be destroyed. Then the second coming of Jesus Christ will be fulfilled. This is the Great Tribulation, the final three-and-a-half years.

Very soon, a new leader will emerge on the scene, a man with great charisma. It could be after a devastating war in the Middle East, where Israel will come out on top; this is the war that Ezekiel forewarn and foretold to Israel. The burden of Damascus in Isaiah 17 could be the out come of this war.

This leader will have a plan to restore peace. Through this plain he will quickly rise to power, captivate, and control the world. It will be easy and very quick for him, because all believers in Jesus Christ will have recently disappeared from earth in the rapture. He will have no trouble persuading most of the remaining people of earth. He will astound and amaze them with feats of supernatural doings, of diplomacy, conquest and much more.

This man (the beast) or (antichrist) will be possessed by Satan in the Great Tribulation part, the last three-and-a-half years. This is right after Satan the devil has been cast down to earth after the war in heaven. Moreover, he will claim to be God; this is when all hell breaks loose on the earth. The first half of the tribulation was bad, but the last three-and-a-half years will be the most terrible times the earth has ever known. The very existence of man is at hand, if it was not stopped, it would result in no life at all.

Before the human race is destroyed, Jesus Christ the king of kings will return and get rid of the impostor who will claim to be God. Jesus will set up his kingdom on earth that will never be destroyed, and Israel will finally have her kingdom. God will live in the midst of this kingdom and there will peace forever and ever.

I am certain that "these things" the events that Jesus said will lead up to the Tribulation will occur during this current generation [us] If you know what to look for you will see signs appearing all around us. If you study God's prophecies to discover all the signs or events, you would see what the future holds for all of us, and you will see many turning points.

Jesus prepared his followers to be able to read the signs of the times. He pointed out it is necessary to understand the meaning of the times, the turning points, the events that are to unfold and to prepare for Jesus at the end of the age. Jesus had a theme, be prepared so we will understand the times we now live in, and so we could have understanding of our own turning points, and to prepare for what lies ahead. We are told to look for certain prophetic developments as they unfold. Jesus called attention to Daniels vision of the antichrist defiling the rebuilt temple in Jerusalem. One of the signs to look for is the temple to be rebuilt in Jerusalem.

In addition, Jesus called attention to this prophetic development for us to know that it will start the Great Tribulation, the last three-and-a-half years of God's wrath. The rebuilt temple will have to build before the Great tribulation, so the Antichrist can fulfill the abomination of desolation prophecies in Daniel,(the desecration and defilement of the temple) is the Antichrist's act of enthroning himself and setting himself as a God himself as God.

The temple in Jerusalem being rebuilt and Israel restoration to the Promised Land is a focal point of the times. These are some of the key turning points we are seeing right now. Remember that Israel is God's source of blessing to the world through the Jew's.

It is important that we recognize the hidden events and trends that are around Israel in the news. We are now witnessing the fulfillment of numerous unique prophecies that are setting the stage for the tribulation and the return of Jesus Christ. Israel is the time line for all this to happen. Jesus declared to believers to have no fear but to fill up with hope for his return.

To date we know the temple has not been rebuilt, I am looking for a war with Israel and the Middle East to happen first, I believe God, will defined Israel, and the Middle East will lose big time. This will let the peace treaty start which will let the temple be rebuilt. Ezekiel was a prophet of God. He foretold the destruction of Jerusalem and the first temple, and the scattering of the Jew's. He also foretold their ultimate return and restoration to the Promised Land. Ezekiel warned Israel of the impending judgment for Israel from whom the glory of God will depart and the Jewish people will be in captivity and scattering among the nations.

Ezekiel warned Israel to repent or God will depart and withdraw His glory from the temple and city of Jerusalem. To repent from all the idols in the house of Israel and worshiping of the sun and much more. It is important to know that the Jewish nation was divided into two tribes at the time of the Babylonian invasion. The two tribes or nations were the northern tribes of Israel and the tribes of Judah. God had reveal that the Jewish people will no longer be divided into two tribes or nations, but will be one when Jesus comes back. When the house of Israel was living in their own land; they defiled it by their ways and their deeds. Therefore God pour out his wrath on them because they had defiled it with their idols God scattered them among the nations.

Ezekiel foretold of a terrible and overwhelming invasion against regathered Israel in the latter years. This amazing prophecy of the Middle East alliance will set the stage for the Antichrist. This alliance of invaders will sweep over the land like a storm, but God will move against the invaders with a great earthquake, pestilence, and rain of fire and brimstone. The invaders will be destroyed. This will be right before the tribulation starts. The rapture could have are ready happened or will very soon after this all starts. This invasion can come at anytime now, because Israel was regathered in 1947 to the Promised Land.

(Eze.39:1-29) That follows is that Invasion, the burden of Damascus is most likely the reason how the invaders will be destroyed. (Isaiah 17) "Behold, Damascus will cease from [being] a city, and it will be a ruinous heap."

{Ezekiel 39:1-29 NLT}-[1] "Son of man, prophesy against Gog. Give him this message from the Sovereign LORD: I am your enemy, O Gog, ruler of the nations of Meshech and Tubal. [2] I will turn you around and drive you toward the mountains of Israel, bringing you from the distant north. [3] I will knock the bow from your left hand and the arrows from your right hand, and I will leave you helpless. [4] You and your army and your allies will all die on the mountains. I will feed you to the vultures and wild animals. [5] You will fall in the open fields, for I have spoken, says the Sovereign LORD. [6] And I will rain down fire on Magog and on all your allies who live safely on the coasts. Then they will know that I am the LORD. [7] "In this way, I will make known my holy name among my people of Israel. I will not let anyone bring shame on it. And the nations, too, will know that I am the LORD, the Holy One of Israel. [8] That day of judgment will come, says the Sovereign LORD. Everything will happen just as I have declared it. [9] "Then the people in the towns of Israel will go out and pick up your small and large shields, bows and arrows, javelins and spears, and they will use them for fuel. There will be enough to last them seven years! [10] They won't need to cut wood from the fields or forests, for these weapons will give them all the fuel they need. They will plunder those who planned to plunder them, and they will rob those who planned to rob them, says the Sovereign LORD. [11] "And I will make a vast graveyard for Gog and his hordes in the Valley of the Travelers, east of the Dead Sea. It will block the way of those who travel there, and they will change the name of the place to the Valley of Gog's Hordes. [12] It will take seven months for the people of Israel to bury the bodies and cleanse the land. [13] Everyone in Israel will help, for it will be a glorious victory for Israel when I demonstrate my glory on that day, says the Sovereign LORD. [14] "After seven months, teams of men will be appointed to search the land for skeletons to bury, so the land will be made clean again. [15] Whenever bones are found, a marker will be set up so the burial crews will take them to be buried in the Valley of Gog's Hordes. [16] (There will be a town there named Hamonah, which means 'horde.') And so the land will finally be cleansed. [17] "And now, son of man, this is what the Sovereign LORD says: Call all the birds and wild animals. Say to them: Gather together for my great sacrificial feast. Come from far and near to the mountains of Israel, and there eat flesh and drink blood! [18] Eat the flesh of mighty men and drink the blood of princes as though they were rams, lambs, goats, and bulls—all fattened animals from Bashan! [19] Gorge yourselves with flesh until you are glutted; drink blood until you are drunk. This is the sacrificial feast I have prepared for you. [20] Feast at my banquet table—feast on horses and charioteers, on mighty men and all kinds of valiant warriors, says the Sovereign LORD. [21] "In this way, I will demonstrate my glory to the nations. Everyone will see the punishment I have inflicted on them and the power of my fist when I strike [22] And from that time on the people of Israel will know that I am the LORD their God. [23] The nations will then know why Israel was sent away to exile—it was punishment for sin, for they were unfaithful to their God. Therefore, I turned away from them and let their enemies destroy them. [24] I turned my face away and punished them because of their defilement and their sins.

[25] "So now, this is what the Sovereign LORD says: I will end the captivity of my people ; I will have mercy on all Israel, for I jealously guard my holy reputation! [26] They will accept responsibility for their past shame and unfaithfulness after they come home to live in peace in their own land, with no one to bother them. [27] When I bring them home from the lands of their enemies, I will display my holiness

among them for all the nations to see. [28] Then my people will know that I am the LORD their God, because I sent them away to exile and brought them home again. I will leave none of my people behind. [29] And I will never again turn my face from them, for I will pour out my Spirit upon the people of Israel. I, the Sovereign LORD, have spoken!"

Isaiah 17:1-14 NKJV}-[1] The burden against Damascus. "Behold, Damascus will cease from [being] a city, And it will be a ruinous heap. [2] The cities of Aroer [are] forsaken; They will be for flocks Which lie down, and no one will make [them] afraid. [3] The fortress also will cease from Ephraim, The kingdom from Damascus, And the remnant of Syria; They will be as the glory of the children of Israel," Says the LORD of hosts. [4] "In that day it shall come to pass [That] the glory of Jacob will wane, And the fatness of his flesh grow lean. [5] It shall be as when the harvester gathers the grain, And reaps the heads with his arm; It shall be as he who gathers heads of grain In the Valley of Rephaim. [6] Yet gleaning grapes will be left in it, Like the shaking of an olive tree, Two [or] three olives at the top of the uppermost bough, Four [or] five in its most fruitful branches," Says the LORD God of Israel. [7] In that day a man will look to his Maker, And his eyes will have respect for the Holy One of Israel. [8] He will not look to the altars, The work

Understanding Your Cross Roads with God's Divine Viewpoint

of his hands; He will not respect what his fingers have made, Nor the wooden images nor the incense altars. [9] In that day his strong cities will be as a forsaken bough And an uppermost branch, Which they left because of the children of Israel; And there will be desolation. [10] Because you have forgotten the God of your salvation, And have not been mindful of the Rock of your stronghold, Therefore you will plant pleasant plants And set out foreign seedlings; [11] In the day you will make your plant to grow, And in the morning you will make your seed to flourish; [But] the harvest [will be] a heap of ruins In the day of grief and desperate sorrow.

[12] Woe to the multitude of many people [Who] make a noise like the roar of the seas, And to the rushing of nations [That] make a rushing like the rushing of mighty waters! [13] The nations will rush like the rushing of many waters; But [God] will rebuke them and they will flee far away, And be chased like the chaff of the mountains before the wind, Like a rolling thing before the whirlwind. [14] Then behold, at eventide, trouble! [And] before the morning, he [is] no more. This [is] the portion of those who plunder us, And the lot of those who rob us.

There will be a leader that will emerge from this invasion, and he will be the lawless one the Antichrist and have great charisma, and is secretly at work and he will remain that way until this invasion takes place and the one holding him back is out of the way. We know what is holding him back, it is the Holy Spirit. We also know that the Holy Spirit is in all believers, so when the Holy Spirit steps out of the way you will have the rapture. The lawlessness one is the Antichrist or beast, and remember Satan will posses him in the final three-and-a-half years of the Great Tribulation. After of the burden of Damascus in Isaiah 17, the people of Israel will turn back to God. This is what it says about Damascus, and then behold, at eventide, trouble! Before the morning, no more.

{Isaiah 17:7-8 NLT}-[7] Then at last the people will look to their Creator and turn their eyes to the Holy One of Israel. [8] They will no longer look to their idols for help or worship what their own hands have made. They will never again bow down to their Asherah poles or worship at the pagan shrines they have built.

{2 Thessalonians 2:4, 6-12 NKJV}-[4] who opposes and exalts himself above all that is called God or that is worshiped, so that he sits as God in the temple of God, showing himself that he is God...[6] And now you know what is restraining, that he may be revealed in his own time. [7] For the mystery of lawlessness is already at work; only He who now restrains [will do so] until He is taken out of the way. [8] And then the lawless one will be revealed, whom the Lord will consume with the breath of His mouth and destroy with the brightness of His coming. [9] The coming of the [lawless one] is according to the working of Satan, with all power, signs, and lying wonders, [10] and with all unrighteous deception among those who perish, because they did not receive the love of the truth, that they might be saved. [11] And for this reason God will send them strong delusion, that they should believe the lie, [12] that they all may be condemned who did not believe the truth but had pleasure in unrighteousness.

In summary then the tribulation will began when the covenant of peace between the coming new world government the Antichrist and the nation of Israel for 7 years. However, halfway through the Tribulation he will break that covenant of peace with Israel, which will start the Great Tribulation, the final three-and-a-half years. This world leader will come out of the war from (Ezekiel) and (Isaiah). The Antichrist will break the covenant by the Abomination of Desolation.

The tribulation will end with the second coming of Jesus Christ. The Antichrist and his false prophet will be seized and thrown alive into the lake of fire, at that time Satan's activity will come to a temporary end. He will be locked in the bottomless pit for the next thousand years. During this time Jesus Christ will set up his thousand-year reign, Jesus reigns from Jerusalem for the next thousand years. At the end of that time, Satan will be set free and he will deceive the nation on the earth once more. Satan will start one more rebellion against God. In that final rebellion, Satan will be supernaturally destroyed by God. At that point, Satan will be thrown into the lake of fire, where the Antichrist and the false prophet and the devils demons are. There they will be tormented day and nigh forever.

CHAPTER 7

THE TURNING POINTS OF THE PROPHETIC TIME CLOCK

Some of the major turning points of the Bible predicts future events; these turning points can give us the big picture of what is to come in the last days. These events are not always clear to us. Therefore, we must be cautious about speculating on what they actually say. We should not try to make the Scriptures of the Bible say more than what they are saying. Our goal should be not to maximizing or minimizing the future events, but to show how they are to come, and to have understanding of these turning points. Daniel's prophecy unlocks God's mysteries plan for Israel and the entire world. The ruler or prince of this world is Satan, and he knows that he has little time. The time for Satan is drawing near to be cast out. The rapture and the tribulation are near very near. The devil will be eviction from heaven in a fit of rage in the Great Tribulation, woe to the inhabitants of the earth. Satan will want to cause as much death and lose of souls as he can at that time.

Daniel's visions of seventy weeks give us a time line for the Jewish people, this is very important for the prophetic time clock. The prophetic time clock is the time God decreed that he would complete His punishment and redemption of the Jewish nation in 490 years (70) weeks. Now God did not say that all 490 years would be in row, it could stop and start at any time. He never said it would be in numeric order. Keep in mind that Daniel's 70 weeks is for Israel. It was given to explain what would happen to them in the latter years. This prophecy provides a chronological key to Bible prophecies. It concerns both the beginning and ending of the punishment for Jerusalem and the Jew's. From the time of the Babylonian conquest to the second coming of Jesus Christ, and defines that period as the times of the Gentiles.

Daniel understood from the prophecies of Jeremiahs that the Babylonian exile would last for 70 years. Daniel expected the restoration to the promise land with the conclusion of the 70 years in exile. However the Archangel Gabriel delivered to him the 70 weeks prophecies, and that revealed that Israel's restoration would be progressive and than fulfilled only at the time of the end.

According to Daniel, six major events characterize the 490 years. They are as followers 1to finish the transgression,2 to put an end to sin,3 and to atone for iniquity,4 to bring in everlasting righteousness,5 to seal both vision and prophet,6 and to anoint a most holy place. These six goals are what God will accomplish during these 70 weeks, or 490 years.

All of this is very confusing but all we have to know is that 490 years are allotted for that prophetic time clock, that God decreed for the six events or goals he set, and for Him to complete his redemption of the Jewish nation. We know that 483 years are fulfilled and that there are 7 years still on that time clock. We know that those 7 years are for the tribulation. God has accuracy fulfilled 483 years on that prophetic time clock just as the Bible has foretold, with 100% accurate to the letter. Only 7 years left on that time clock for the tribulation you can bet that it will be fulfilled to the letter.

One the greatest prophecies of all times has been fulfilled in recent years, the restoration of the Jewish nation to the Promised Land. Remember Jesus stated that the generation that sees these things begin would not pass from the scene until all is completed. Israel became a nation in 1947, over 64 years since the

Jewish nation was restored to the Promised Land. (From the time of this writing) Surely, Jesus Christ return is very near. That generation that sees all these things occur will not cease to exist until all the future events of the tribulation are literally fulfilled. The generation from1947 may not pass until all is completed and all seceding generations from that time on. The generation that sees these signs happen will see the end happen. The only question is how long a generation in the Bible is. The bible gives 40 years to 120 for a generation, but do not put a time on it, to see when it will all end.

Remember only God knows the day and time but, we know the beginning was in 1947. The Antichrist will offer peace to the world after the war of (Ezekiel 39:1-29). He will make a covenant of peace with Israel. This will aloud for the temple to be rebuild and to reinstate their Jewish sacrifices again. This covenant is for 7 years and 3.5 years will elapsed then the Antichrist will bring an end to sacrifice and offerings to God. He will set him self-up as God, and the Antichrist will break his covenant with the Jew's in the middle of the tribulation and will make his desolation, the abomination of desolation. This will start what we call the Great Tribulation time period. His army will take over the temple.

As the end times signs continue to multiply the Devil knows and realizes that time is fast approaching when he will be able to physically manifest himself as God of this world. He will anoint the lawless one and then possess him; this man the Bible calls the beast or the Antichrist. While the Antichrist is doing, Satan will, consolidating worldwide an empire into a one-world government. Satan will try to seize the throne of God. This is the war in heaven in the middle of the tribulation, when Satan will be cast down to earth. He will be cut off completely from heaven. Then Satan will take out his anger on the chosen people of God. This is the Great Tribulation part of the tribulation the last half 3.5 years. Satan will possess the beast and enter the rebuilt Jewish temple, and declare himself to be God. He will demand that the entire world worship him.

Remember Satan is released from the bottomless pit, and he deceives many into joining him. However, Satan is cast into the lake of fire. At that time, all unsaved dead of all time will appear before the Great White Throne. All who have lived through history regardless of their stature or position, which have died with out acknowledging and accepting Jesus Christ payment for sin. Whether in the earth, sea, mausoleum, remains of ashes will be raised and united with their souls and spirits so they can stand at the

Great White Throne. The soul of the believer is in the presence of God, awaiting eternal reward. The soul of the unbeliever is in Hades, the place of the wicked and dead, awaiting judgment at the Great White Throne Judgment. The resurrection of the unsaved occurs at the end of history, the end of the millennial kingdom. The lost of all ages will be collected from the place of Hades, and be brought before The Great White Throne. Here they will be condemned to spend eternity in the lake of fire.

{Revelation 20:9-15 NKJV}-[9] They went up on the breadth of the earth and surrounded the camp of the saints and the beloved city. And fire came down from God out of heaven and devoured them. [10] The devil, who deceived them, was cast into the lake of fire and brimstone where the beast and the false prophet [are]. And they will be tormented day and night forever and ever. [11] Then I saw a great white throne and Him who sat on it, from whose face the earth and the heaven fled away. And there was found no place for them. [12] And I saw the dead, small and great, standing before God, and books were opened. And another book was opened, which is [the Book] of Life. And the dead were judged according to their works, by the things that were written in the books. [13] The sea gave up the dead who were in it, and Death and Hades delivered up the dead who were in them. And they were judged, each one according to his works. [14] Then Death and Hades were cast into the lake of fire. This is the second death. [15] And anyone not found written in the Book of Life was cast into the lake of fire.

The final rebellion against God will be the climax of the millennial kingdom of Jesus Christ. When the thousand years are over, Satan will be released from his prison and will go out to deceive the nations in the four corners of earth. He will gather those who still will want to sin, and will be joining him in battle. They will be like the sand on the seashore in number. They will surrounded God's people, and the city he loves. However, fire will comes down from heaven and devoured them. This battle will be the last battle ever to be. That battle will be at the end of the millennial kingdom and Satan's final attempt to conquer the world. There will be no dead bodies they will be consumed by fire from God. Then the Great White Throne judgment will begin. At the end of the Great White Throne, judgment there will be a new heaven, new earth, and New Jerusalem, and they will be quite different from our present ones. The book of revelation focusing on the new Holy City of Jerusalem, instead of the new heaven and earth.

A good point here is that there has never been a world ruler who made a covenant for peace that was for 7 years with Israel, and then brakes that covenant 3.5 years into it. The Jerusalem temple has not been rebuilt to date. Therefore, the Antichrist can make that abomination of desolation. These events will occur in that 7-years that are still on that prophetic time clock and will be the time we call the tribulation.

The Bible states that a person dies only once and after that comes judgment, so also Christ died only once as a sacrifice to take away the sins of many people. He will come again but not to deal with our sins. This time he will bring salvation to all those who are eagerly waiting for him. The scriptures here states that judgment will follow death. Nevertheless, our status with Jesus determines how we are to be judged. Remember following the rapture, the believers will stand before the judgment seat of Jesus Christ. However, this is far, very far different from what will happen to the unbeliever who will appear before the Great White Throne judgment at the end of the 1000 years reign of Christ.

The resurrection of the unsaved occurs at the end of history. The lost of all ages will be collected from the place of Hades, and be brought before The Great White Throne. Here they will be condemned to spend eternity in the lake of fire. Have you invited Christ in your life to forgive your sins and save your soul? If you have not done so now is a good time to do so. You may say I am not sure, I am in between, but I do not want to go through the tribulation or follow the Antichrist. So why not do so now? Go ahead and ask God to help, you will not lose anything if you do. However, if you wait to long,…you know the lake of fire awaits for you

Our Lord said, "He who is not with me is against me." There is no middle ground. There is only 7 years to go on that prophetic time clock. It can start at anytime now and could have since 1947. If you would like to miss the 21 judgments of the tribulation and God's wrath, it is up to you, how you make your choice rapture or tribulation. Do you want to be fooled by Satan and on your way to the day of destruction? Do you still refuse to believe the truth that can save you, and do you want to be thrown into the lake of fire? You can make the right choice here and now, go ahead and chose your salvation.

CHAPTER 8

WHERE ARE WE NOW ON THAT PROPHETIC TIME CLOCK

{Ezekiel 36:16-28 NLT}-[16] Then this further message came to me from the LORD: [17] "Son of man, when the people of Israel were living in their own land, they defiled it by the evil way they lived. To me their conduct was as unclean as a woman's menstrual cloth. [18] They polluted the land with murder and the worship of idols, so I poured out my fury on them. [19] I scattered them to many lands to punish them for the evil way they had lived. [20] But when they were scattered among the nations, they brought shame on my holy name. For the nations said, 'These are the people of the LORD, but he couldn't keep them safe in his own land!' [21] Then I was concerned for my holy name, on which my people brought shame among the nations. [22] "Therefore, give the people of Israel this message from the Sovereign LORD: I am bringing you back, but not because you deserve it. I am doing it to protect my holy name, on which you brought shame while you were scattered among the nations. [23] I will show how holy my great name is— the name on which you brought shame among the nations. And when I reveal my holiness through you before their very eyes, says the Sovereign LORD, then the nations will know that I am the LORD. [24] For I will gather you up from all the nations and bring you home again to your land. [25] "Then I will sprinkle clean water on you, and you will be clean. Your filth will be washed away, and you will no longer worship idols. [26] And I will give you a new heart, and I will put a new spirit in you. I will take out your stony, stubborn heart and give you a tender, responsive heart. [27] And I will put my Spirit in you so that you will follow my decrees and be careful to obey my regulations. [28] "And you will live in Israel, the land I gave your ancestors long ago. You will be my people, and I will be your God.

Where are we now on that prophetic time clock, and what turning points are we to consider coming, and how close are we to the end? Remember that Ezekiel foretold of a terrible and overwhelming invasion against regathered Israel in the latter years. Therefore, we can presume that turning point of prophecy about the Middle East alliance will set the stage for the Antichrist to come. In addition, we should expect the burdensome stone that Zechariah predicted to intensify and become more and more intense. In addition, we can look for Damascus to be no more, and then behold, at eventide, trouble! Before the morning, no more. So the one sure answer that I can give, we are now closer to the end than we have ever been. However, only God has the ultimate answer to that question. No one except God knows for sure how close we are.

We can point to various turning points-such as the regathering of Israel to her promise land, and looking for the wars that Ezekiel and Isaiah foretold, the continued tensions in the Middle East, the development of a one-world economy that the Antichrist could easily controlled. I can confidently say, the rapture may come today, but at the same time, I must also admit that it may not come until we are in the next decade. The scripture most often used to pinpoint the coming of Jesus Christ is Matthew 24.

{Matthew 24:32-38 NASB}-[32] "Now learn the parable from the fig tree: when its branch has already become tender and puts forth its leaves, you know that summer is near; [33] so, you too, when you see all these things, recognize that He is near, right at the door. [34] "Truly I say to you, this generation will not pass away until all these things take place. [35]

"Heaven and earth will pass away, but My words will not pass away. [36] "But of that day and hour no one knows, not even the angels of heaven, nor the Son, but the Father alone. [37] "For the coming of the Son of Man will be just like the days of Noah. [38] "For as in those days before the flood they were eating and drinking, marrying and giving in marriage, until the day that Noah entered the ark,

    I too use this verse to prove we are in the time of the end the last days. However, this probably means that the tribulation period, will not pass away before Jesus Christ returns. This generation means the generation that personally witnesses all of the turning points, thus this scripture should not be used to establish a date for the rapture, tribulation or the coming of Jesus Christ. However those of us who see the turning points on the horizon, all we can say is that we believe we are in the last days in a general sense. We do recognize the prophetic significance of these turning points. The point is that we are to live as these turning points could come at any moment.

    What should we be doing if Jesus Christ is coming soon? We should consistently be on the lookout for turning points for His coming. The scriptures in 1 Peter's 4:7-10 gives clear and practical advice of what we should be doing. And, the scriptures tells to be earnest in other words, we should be characterized by showing deep sincerity or by being honest. We are to be clearheaded and alert for seeing these cross roads. Be mentally alert and disciplined for a life of prayer. As we see these cross roads approaching, we are to love one another. One of the many cross roads that Jesus use was the love of many would turn cold in the last days. We are to show warmth to strangers, and open our home. We are to use our spiritual gifts to serve one another; every believer in Jesus Christ is giving at least one spiritual gift.

{1 Peter 4:7-10 NASB}-[7] The end of all things is near; therefore, be of sound judgment and sober spirit for the purpose of prayer. [8] Above all, keep fervent in your love for one another, because love covers a multitude of sins. [9] Be hospitable to one another without complaint. [10] As each one has received a special gift, employ it in serving one another as good stewards of the manifold grace of God.

Do not be afraid or intimidated by the turning points of 2012. God wants you to understand and apply these to your life. God has promised a blessing to you if you do. By following, these turning points and asking God to open your heart and mind to them you will have understanding of them. This scripture is saying that the end of the world is coming; therefore, here is what we should be doing. As we approach the apocalypse of 2012, more and more people are going to be caught up in the frenzy. Some people will be tempted to quit their jobs, and sell all they have. But as I have said 2012 is not what you need to be ready for you must get right with the Lord. So forget 2012 and all the domes day Sayers. Prepare yourself for the last days. Time is short we are in the last days that the Bible talks about. As the scriptures says, the end is near. The scriptures talk about the time of the season, know that we are in the season that Jesus gave an illustration on, (Matthew 24:32-34 NLT} above.

The Bible gives us numerous turning points and signs to watch for, that indicate whether or not if we are living in the last days. By seeing these turning points, we know we are in the season. The number one turning point that I believe was when Israel was regathered and restored. It began in 1948 and continues to be going on today as the Jews are being brought back to their promise land. Israel must exist as an independent nation for many prophecies to be fulfilled. One key prophecy is the burdensome stone; Israel must be a nation for the world to be involved with Israel and the Jews. It is interesting that Israel seems to be in the news every day now; all eyes are on this tiny state, the peace process of the Middle East swirls around it.

The birth of the nation of Israel and the restoration from Babylonian &Persian captivity, and its continued survival is a miracle. Israel has survived four all-out wars—1948-49, 1956, 1967, and 1973. These wars were the combined might of Islam for the purpose of annihilating Israel. Can you see a pattern here, and remember Israel had to regained control of its ancient capital city of Jerusalem for some prophecies to be fulfilled. The Middle East will ignite a global war, all the nations of the earth will be gathered for war, and the result will be Armageddon.

We are living in the last days, so it is not surprising that Israel is in the news much of the time, the burdensome stone that Zechariah predicted. Jerusalem has become that burdensome stone for the world. Moreover, it is not surprising that present day Iraq, Iran, and Syria is the focus of international tension. Jesus prepared His followers to see the turning points that we are now seeing. He pointed out that in the midst of world upheaval, that it is necessary to understand the meaning of these key developments. In addition, Jesus said these upheaval and tensions would be a signal the final countdown to Apocalypse.

Jesus called our attention to Daniel's prophecy about the Antichrist defiling the rebuilt Temple in Jerusalem. So based on this information it is very likely the figure known as the Antichrist has already been born and is an adult. We do not know the name of him, but somehow his name will be connected with the mystical number 666. Very soon, he will arise and become visible on the global scene, and gradually position himself as a politically leader, later he will take political control of much of the world. The Antichrist will consolidate most of the political, economic, and military power on a scale never seen before. He will rise through a confederation of European and Mediterranean nations. This is the revival of the ancient Roman Empire, which Daniel foretold.

Here are just some of the major turning points on that prophetic time clock.1 The Antichrist will become a world dictator,2 and the ancient Roman Empire will be revived, 3 a seven-year treaty or covenant with Israel and this will prove to be a false treaty,4 the mark of the beast a totalitarian police system whereby every person will be tracked, 5 the mark of the beast will be the number 666 and all who accept the mark will acknowledge their submission to the Antichrist, 6 the world will have devastating battles and wars which will lead to the cataclysmic war of Armageddon,7 the drying up of the Euphrates River which is now very possible due to the construction of a huge dam in Turkey the Atatuurk and it will be able to cut off the flow o the headwaters and much more.

CHAPTER 9

THE WORLD TOMORROW

Man wants desperately to save his society-the civilization he has established upon the earth. This civilization cannot be saved! Man, he is bringing this world to and end. God almighty will soon step in, and create a new peaceful and happy society. You do not have to believe it! It will happen just as the Bible has said. Regardless of what you might think! It is certain as the rising of tomorrow's sun. Man will not bring it about-it is going to be done to us. This is not a pipe dream; humanity is going to be forced to enjoy God's Utopia. Man is going to enjoy word peace and universal joy, which will fill the earth. Utopia, yes and there is cause for today's world chaos and threat of human extinction. Just take a look at today's world evils, its trends, and conditions of this sick, sick world that we live in.

Why today's world evils? How can today's trends unleash a Utopia upon the world? How can it all end in peace? What will cause this world to erupt into peace and love? In addition, what will this world (the earth) be like? How will it be governed? Who will rule? How will such incredible change be brought about? In addition, what will this Utopia be like? What really is ahead and why? What is actually going to be the outcome of this divided sick-sick world? The outcome is something totally unseen by world leaders and scientists, educators and more.

Many world leaders and scientists and many educated people, now expect that nuclear destruction eventually very-soon will erase human life from this earth. Besides nuclear annihilation, there are other means by which humankind could be destroyed. Biological warfare, overpopulation, disease epidemics, and environmental pollution are just a few to mention. Consider these facts; Human life is sustained by air, water, and food. Man today is polluting his life-sustained supply of these necessities at a fast rate and it seems to be accelerating. Air pollution and fall out from nuclear waste is not only threatening mans life, but is render plant life sick. Many rivers and lakes worldwide have been so seriously polluted that the water supply in many places are at a crisis stage. Man has depleted and ruined the soil. In addition, erosion caused by floods has ruined the soil. Food factories extract life-sustaining minerals and vitamins out of the food. Worldwide weather in droughts and floods are resulting in mass starvation in some parts of the world, and brings epidemics and disease.

These are the evils of man and are fast accelerating, if these evils do not destroy humanity soon, some of the experts say that the population explosion can and will. As global population soars, the world resources is threatening to become even more depleted, the imbalance of human numbers and rapidly dwindling life-sustaining resources shows us that the world cannot adequately care for the overpopulation.

Leading scientists look around and say they are frankly frightened. They warn us that our hope lies in a pipe-dream, the only way out for them is a super world government, capable of uniteniting us, and acting on all these problems on a global scale. This widely held view of the future offers no hope. Some of these scientists admittedly say it is impossible for a world government. How can nations hostile against one another from such a government? In addition, the people in authority would not be able to cope with the worlds evils that threatens mans civilization that he has established upon this earth than present leaders.

These people dangled before our eyes a glittering, glamour world of technology, world of their making.

A push-button dream world of leisure and luxury. They are working to convert this world into a material world, and covert this world into heaven on earth. Ignoring the realty and conditions described just above. How ironic tends oscillate between an extreme of gloom or a world of glittering and luxury. How true that those voicing the most glamorous predictions seem to totally exclude world conditions and seem unable to comprehend the snarls and problems of their own predictions. However, does this kind of society sound truly good to you? Think of the many problems they would create, rather than solve. Yet millions anticipate such developments, hopefully in their own lifetime, while not respecting other scientists who see impending doom.

The man made Utopian has the same patterns and consequences as does the gloom and doom. Many will be satisfied with a Utopian world, but some would find life meaningless and purposeless. For the gloom and doom the average mans life will deteriorate. People will be more poorly fed and every attempt to improve their situation would be wiped out by the continued population. Some would be satisfied but most would find life meaningless and purposeless. Not very good or happy predictions are they.

So now you can see the two opposite views of scientists and leaders and educators, one of gloom and hopeless, and one of progress and of luxury. Nevertheless, both are wrong and these concepts are false. God will soon create a new peaceful and happy society. Jesus Christ will set up His kingdom on earth. Jesus Christ is about to break out into the open with his rule and set up his kingdom for 1000 years. We can all be saved no matter what we have done. We are made right in God's sight when we believe his promise to take away our sins. All we have to do is trust in Jesus Christ and call on his name. For all have sinned and are falling short of God's standard. There is only one path that leads to God. There is only one God, and there is only one way of being accepted. Moreover, that way makes our sins go away by faith in Jesus Christ.

When we take a long hard realistic look at the conditions and trends of today, they do have turning points that point to a fast-approaching world crisis of combined nuclear war, starvation, disease and epidemics, crime and violence and the end to human life. Before we look at what God has said in the Bible, and what is actually going to come we need to look at this world and the civilization man has established upon the earth. We need to look at education and science technology, industry, governments, and the social order and yes religion.

Why education? Today's world is what its leaders have made it. In addition, the leaders are the product of modern education. It is a system by which the leaders inject their philosophies mans, and not God's. Education is essentially pagan in origin and character. They inject their ideas, customs, and culture into the minds of there generation. The academic system is believed to be founded by the pagan philosopher Plato. There is a drift into materialism and God is ignored.

Modern education teaches students to earn a living but fails to teach them how to live with each other. We find false values, and the teaching of distorted history, warped psychology, perverted arts, and worthless knowledge. I would like to say not all higher education is like this. God calls this materialistic world of knowledge foolishness. What has caused this foolishness? A mixed-up, unhappy, and fearful world in chaos. Moreover, human knowledge without God is confined to this physical and material world. True values of mans purpose and life and the way to peace, prosperity, happiness, abundant living is made possible only through the Holy Spirit.

{1 Corinthians 3:18-20 NASB}-[18] Let no man deceive himself. If any man among you thinks that he is wise in this age, he must become foolish, so that he may become wise. [19] For the wisdom of this world is foolishness before God. For it is written, "He is THE ONE WHO CATCHES THE WISE IN THEIR CRAFTINESS"; [20] and again, "THE LORD KNOWS THE REASONINGS of the wise, THAT THEY ARE USELESS."

Today's world looks to science and technology to deliver it from these worlds evils and solve all its problems. It is the magic button for some. However, modern science can not reveal to the world the purpose of human life or explain its true meaning. It remains ignorant to the truth, it does not know the way to peace. You can only get the truth from God, if science chooses to ignore God ways it is wise by this world's standards and not the standards that God has set up for us to live by. It has failed miserably to deliver the world from poverty, famine, disease, worries, and unhappiness and has not rid the world of any of its evils.

Commerce and industry is based on competition and greed, marketing their products or services to vanity and wrong desires. They use dishonesty, misrepresentation, deception to get what they want. It is a competition to the top and has selfish motivation and not the public good at interest or concern for others that would bring happiness to this world. The politicians in government are said to be in public service and are in offices of authority and power. They have the power to regulate society and guide it; they have made what the world is today. To many of those who seek offices of power over the people promise great benefits and to service the people but their motives are ambitions for personal power and wealth. The modern forms of government promises peace, happiness, and prosperity to its own people. We find secret deals, and dishonesty running rampant in high places of today's modern government. Government promises are empty. We the people are pawns who give the government money in order to get part of it back. In modern government, we fail to find any knowledge of life's purpose or the truth. Modern government is controlled by its sinful nature.

{1 Corinthians 3:3 NLT}-[3] for you are still controlled by your sinful nature. You are jealous of one another and quarrel with each other. Doesn't that prove you are controlled by your sinful nature? Aren't you living like people of the world?

Mankind has struggled from the dawn of civilization with social order. People think of social order as civilization, and civilization as a well order human society that is good, even to the point of perfection. Perhaps you have accepted this popular assumption. The government wants you to accept it. When you limit government power, you expand individual freedom. When it expands, it begins to impose it social order on the people. The law then becomes a tool in which the government can remain in power and impose their will on the people. Social order is said to be human progress, but is civilization really good? Surely social order ought to be good, but is civilization a proud monument in human progress? Look what progress civilization has made, illiteracy, ignorance, unbelievable poverty, filth and squalor and much much more. Is all this worth preserving? Do you find life purpose and true meaning of happiness in the social order we have?

We have class distinctions, racial discrimination, religious bigotry, and selfish motives from our social order and civilization and this is human progress? This world's civilization is mentally, morally, and spiritually sick. It is as if civilization is making progress in reverse, and is now bring about its own destruction. Nevertheless, the future is not hopeless. This evil world is to be replaced very soon with Jesus Christ kingdom.

What has religion done for us? We should expect to find at last hope and the true knowledge of life purpose in one of the world religion. However, here we find the most sickening disillusionment of all. We find reluctantly that much of today's religion is following pagan customs. Some established religious organizations, which profess the name of Jesus Christ, are teaching the opposite of his teachings. Much of the churches in the Western world is divided and confusion. The churches have not reformed the whole world as they profess they have done, they have failed miserably. In addition, some churches have thrown out the main source of the word of God the bible. They use the culture of our time and they use that culture to get you to absorb it, it is water down religion and seen only through mans eye.

You must proclaim the world of God and Jesus Christ Gospel. In addition, that Jesus is the Christ, the son of God. Some do this but preach only about the person of Jesus Christ and not his Gospel, the good news, which God sent for all of mankind. The gospel of Jesus is not base on human reasoning.

{Matthew 4:23 NASB}-[23] Jesus was going throughout all Galilee, teaching in their synagogues and proclaiming the gospel of the kingdom, and healing every kind of disease and every kind of sickness among the people.

{2 Corinthians 11:4 NLT}-[4] You happily put up with whatever anyone tells you, even if they preach a different Jesus than the one we preach, or a different kind of Spirit than the one you received, or a different kind of gospel than the one you believed

{Galatians 1:8-12 NLT}-[8] Let God's curse fall on anyone, including us or even an angel from heaven, who preaches a different kind of Good News than the one we preached to you. [9] I say again what we have said before: If anyone preaches any other Good News than the one you welcomed, let that person be cursed. [10] Obviously, I'm not trying to win the approval of people, but of God. If pleasing people were my goal, I would not be Christ's servant. [11] Dear brothers and sisters, I want you to understand that the gospel message I preach is not based on mere human reasoning. [12] I received my message from no human source, and no one taught me. Instead, I received it by direct revelation from Jesus Christ.

When we take a realistic view of our modern systems of education, science and technology, commerce and industry, and government, civilization, and our religious faith we find that it was all swayed by Satan.

Yes, Satan has his hand in every thing. In addition, we have found them all full of evil and wrong. Look at the 20th century progress and what is the actual state of the world today? When we take a hard realistic view of conditions and trends, they do point to a fast approaching world crisis. Man has no solution, the more we try, and the more destructive are our efforts. Satan, who is the god of this world, has control over all modern systems, which is why man can never fix the world.

{2 Corinthians 4:3-4 NLT}-[3] If the Good News we preach is hidden behind a veil, it is hidden only from people who are perishing. [4] Satan, who is the god of this world, has blinded the minds of those who don't believe. They are unable to see the glorious light of the Good News. They don't understand this message about the glory of Christ, who is the exact likeness of God.

Utopia is soon to take over this world, in our time and we shall see world peace and find the true meaning of man. Moreover, what will this utopia be like? We shall see sickness banished, ignorance replaced with love and much more. Incredible yes, but that is God's plain for us, when Jesus Christ sets up his kingdom on earth. We need to face it, either there does exist a living God of supreme power who very soon will step in and intervene in the affairs of man and save us from our-self, or else the threatened extinction picture above must soon take place.

Man wants desperately to save his civilization, He has always dreamed of a utopia on earth. He has aspire to create a great society, a paradise on earth, a return to the Garden of Eden. Nevertheless, clearly, man's sinful nature can never produce such a place. Paradise was lost, and man can never hope to on his own regain it.

God's word the Holy Scriptures tells us that after the second coming, Jesus will establish a paradise on earth, His thousand-year reign of glory to God and pace (the millennial kingdom). This kingdom will bring about the complete fulfillment of all God has promised. The scriptures of the Holy Bible has foretold today's world conditions and trends, and gave us advance new of this world and the coming peace on earth. This is good news and is absolutely sure to come about. It is sure because it does not depend on man, God is going to do it, in spite of mans rebellious ways.

Satan is leading us in to a world crisis, where he can take control of our civilization. Our world trends are pointing to a fast approaching time where if God did not step in no human life would be left on earth. God created Lucifer as an archangel and super being, perfect in all his ways, until by his own free will, iniquity was found in him. Lucifer turned to rebellion against God and His ways. To be filled with vanity, lust, and greed. Now Lucifer became know as Satan the devil. The first man Adam, after Satan got to him though his wife Eve, turned to the ways of Satan. This is the curse we are all under now. Adam and Eve, by making the wrong decision acquire Satan attitude. Moreover, all their children the entire human race has acquired it, with the single exception of Jesus Christ.

{Romans 5:12-13 NLT}-[12] When Adam sinned, sin entered the world. Adam's sin brought death, so death spread to everyone, for everyone sinned. [13] Yes, people sinned even before the law was given. But it was not counted as sin because there was not yet any law to break.

{Romans 5:12-21 NKJV}-[12] Therefore, just as through one man sin entered the world, and death through sin, and thus death spread to all men, because all sinned—[13] (For until the law sin was in the world, but sin is not imputed when there is no law. [14] Nevertheless death reigned from Adam to Moses, even over those who had not sinned according to the likeness of the transgression of Adam, who is a type of Him who was to come. [15] But the free gift [is] not like the offense. For if by the one man's offense many died, much more the grace of God and the gift by the grace of the one Man, Jesus Christ, abounded to many. [16] And the gift [is] not like [that which came] through the one who sinned. For the judgment [which came] from one [offense resulted] in condemnation, but the free gift [which came] from many offenses [resulted] in justification. [17] For if by the one man's offense death reigned through the one, much more those who receive abundance of grace and of the gift of righteousness will reign in life through the One, Jesus Christ.) [18] Therefore, as through one man's offense [judgment came] to all men, resulting in condemnation, even so through one Man's righteous act [the free gift came] to all men, resulting in justification of life. [19] For as by one man's disobedience many were made sinners, so also by one Man's obedience many will be made righteous. [20] Moreover the law entered that the offense might abound. But where sin abounded, grace abounded much more, [21] so that as sin reigned in death, even so grace might reign through righteousness to eternal life through Jesus Christ our Lord.

By turning from sin and recognizing the truth, the Law of Moses is a curse, we can not live by the law, and so we sin and live by human nature. God has given us great and precious promises. These are some the promises that enable you to share his divine nature and escape the world's corruption caused by human desires. (Satan nature) Read all of them!

{Romans 8:1-39 NLT}-[1] So now there is no condemnation for those who belong to Christ Jesus. [2] And because you belong to him, the power of the life-giving Spirit has freed you from the power of sin that leads to death. [3] The law of Moses was unable to save us because of the weakness of our sinful nature. So God did what the law could not do. He sent his own Son in a body like the bodies we sinners have. And in that body God declared an end to sin's control over us by giving his Son as a sacrifice for our sins. [4] He did this so that the just requirement of the law would be fully satisfied for us, who no longer follow our sinful nature but instead follow the Spirit. [5] Those who are dominated by the sinful nature think about sinful things, but those who are controlled by the Holy Spirit think about things that please the Spirit. [6] So letting your sinful nature control your mind leads to death. But letting the Spirit control your mind leads to life and peace. [7] For the sinful nature is always hostile to God. It never did obey God's laws, and it never will. [8] That's why those who are still under the control of their sinful nature can never please God. [9] But you are not controlled by your sinful nature. You are controlled by the Spirit if you have the Spirit of God living in you. (And remember that those who do not have the Spirit of Christ living in them do not belong to him at all.) [10] And Christ lives within you, so even though your body will die because of sin, the Spirit gives you life because you have been made right with God. [11] The Spirit of God, who raised Jesus from the dead, lives in you. And just as God raised Christ Jesus from the dead, he will give life to your mortal bodies by this same Spirit living within you. [12] Therefore, dear brothers and sisters, you have no obligation to do what your sinful nature urges you to do. [13] For if you live by its dictates, you will die. But if through the power of the Spirit you put to death the deeds of your sinful nature, you will live. [14] For all who are led by the Spirit of God are children of God. [15] So you have not received a spirit that makes you fearful slaves. Instead, you received God's Spirit when he adopted you as his own children. Now we call him, "Abba, Father." [16] For his Spirit joins with our spirit to affirm that we are God's children. [17] And since we are his children, we are his heirs. In fact, together with Christ we are heirs of God's glory. But if we are to share his glory, we must also share his suffering. [18] Yet what we suffer now is nothing compared to the glory he will reveal to us later. [19] For all creation is waiting eagerly for that future day when God will reveal who his children really are. [20]

Against its will, all creation was subjected to God's curse. But with eager hope, [21] the creation looks forward to the day when it will join God's children in glorious freedom from death and decay. [22] For we know that all creation has been groaning as in the pains of childbirth right up to the present time. [23] And we believers also groan, even though we have the Holy Spirit within us as a foretaste of future glory, for we long for our bodies to be released from sin and suffering. We, too, wait with eager hope for the day when God will give us our full rights as his adopted children, including the new bodies he has promised us. [24] We were given this hope when we were saved. (If we already have something, we don't need to hope for it. [25] But if we look forward to something we don't yet have, we must wait patiently and confidently.) [26] And the Holy Spirit helps us in our weakness. For example, we don't know what God wants us to pray for. But the Holy Spirit prays for us with groanings that cannot be expressed in words. [27] And the Father who knows all hearts knows what the Spirit is saying, for the Spirit pleads for us believers in harmony with God's own will. [28] And we know that God causes everything to work together for the good of those who love God and are called according to his purpose for them. [29] For God knew his people in advance, and he chose them to become like his Son, so that his Son would be the firstborn among many brothers and sisters. [30] And having chosen them, he called them to come to him. And having called them, he gave them right standing with himself. And having given them right standing, he gave them his glory. [31] What shall we say about such wonderful things as these? If God is for us, who can ever be against us? [32] Since he did not spare even his own Son but gave him up for us all, won't he also give us everything else? [33] Who dares accuse us whom God has chosen for his own? No one—for God himself has given us right standing with himself. [34] Who then will condemn us? No one—for Christ Jesus died for us and was raised to life for us, and he is sitting in the place of honor at God's right hand, pleading for us. [35] Can anything ever separate us from Christ's love? Does it mean he no longer loves us if we have trouble or calamity, or are persecuted, or hungry, or destitute, or in danger, or threatened with death? [36] (As the Scriptures say, "For your sake we are killed every day; we are being slaughtered like sheep.") [37] No, despite all these things, overwhelming victory is ours through Christ, who loved us. [38] And I am convinced that nothing can ever separate us from God's love. Neither death nor life, neither angels nor demons, neither our fears for today nor our worries about tomorrow—not even the powers of hell can separate us from God's love. [39] No power in the sky above or in the earth below—indeed, nothing in all creation will ever be able to separate us from the love of God that is revealed in Christ Jesus our Lord.

God is coming to rule by divine force! What a travesty that this earth will be forced to be happy and have abundantly love and joy. We will never have pace and love, until Satan is removed, and human nature is changed. Only God can do that, but that is precisely what Jesus Christ is going to do when He returns to rule over all the Nations of the earth. We must acquire the Divine Nature of God, to be like Him. We must come to real repentance and believe in Jesus Christ, to be partakers of that Divine Nature.

CHAPTER 10

SATAN THE GOD OF THIS WORLD

{2 Corinthians 4:4 NLT}-[4] Satan, who is the god of this world, has blinded the minds of those who don't believe. They are unable to see the glorious light of the Good News. They don't understand this message about the glory of Christ, who is the exact likeness of God.

The Morning Star, Dragon, Serpent, Devil, Satan, Lucifer, The Man of sin, The Accuser, The Deceiver, The Destroyer. These are some of the names that are given in the Bible for the Devil. The Serpent was the shrewdest of all the creatures God made. The Devil is so cunning and shrewd that he tricked the woman Eve into sin. He had her eat of the tree that God said not to do, eat of the tree of good and evil. God said to the serpent because you have done this you are cursed, on your belly you shall go, and you will eat dust all the days of you life. God said to the woman I will multiply your sorrow, and at conception in pain you shall bring forth children and you husband shall rule over you. God calls her woman because Adam had not named her yet.

God sent Adam and Eve out of the garden of Eden, to till the ground from which Adam was taken. God said, "The people have become as we, knowing everything, both good and evil. What if they eat the fruit of the tree of life? Then they will live forever. After banishing them from the garden, the LORD God stationed mighty angelic beings to the east of Eden. In addition, a flaming sword flashed back and forth, guarding the way to the tree of life.

Satan was created by God before the creation of the earth. In Job. 38:4-God asked Job where were you when I laid the foundations of the earth, as the morning stars sang together and all the angels see it says all the angels that would include Satan. Satan chose to rebel against God. Pride caused his downfall and a third of the angelic host. Satan fall must have taken place between the time creation was finished and Adam and Eve were tempted. Because God had pounced all of his work excellent in every way. Adam had time to give names to all of God's creatures before Eve's temptation.

Lucifer became Satan when he fell; his downfall is the greatest example of failure of all time. He was created by God to perfection, and to serve God directly in his Holy Temple. Despite is perfect place he chose to rebellion against God. The earth was created for man. God granted dominion over to Adam and Eve. God said; let them have dominion over the fish of the sea, and over the birds of the air, and over the cattle, and over all the earth, and over every creeping thing that creeps upon the earth.

Though temptation Adam and Eve lost dominion over the earth to Satan, he stole it, he tricked them. This is how Satan could legitimately tempt Jesus Christ by offering him all the kingdoms of the earth.

Satan is a spirit being and a very super one. He is the prince of the power of the air. He is the spirit at work in the hearts of those who refuse to obey God. He the devil—the commander of the powers in the unseen world. Satan, the devil, who is the god of this world, has blinded the minds of those who do not believe. Satan transmits through the air broadcast his attitudes, impulses, desire of vanity and greed, jealousy, envy and any other evil you can think of. Those who do not believe are the sons of disobedience, and Satan spirit works in these sons.

Every human has, from birth a spirit. The human spirit does not think, but it empowers the physical brain to think. The human spirit does not sub-stain life, life is sub-stain by the physical breath of air and food and our blood. The spirit is not human nature, human nature is a cruse through Adam and Eve, it is acquired after birth, we acquire Satan's nature through the brain, and knowledge (good or bad) enters the brain through the five senses, hearing, tasting, smelling, feeling, and seeing. However, the brain cannot use the five senses to feel or see the spirit.

The brain is confined to physical knowledge. Yet the knowledge that enters the physical brain is automatically programmed into the human spirit. Satan uses his spirit to broadcast his nature into the human spirit. Nevertheless, we are under no obligation to do what our human nature urges us to do. We are automatically tuned into Satan's wavelength and nature and attitude, he does broadcast to our spirit and attempts to instill his nature. However, every human is a free spirit, a moral agent, responsible for his or hers own spirit and attitudes, decisions and action. If the human sprint is willing, it will accept and yield to Satan's evil attitudes. Satan has no power over our human spirit, he cannot force any human mind to submit to his nature and attitude, he does broadcast to our spirit, but we have free will to submit or not. Just like, we have free will to partaker of God's Divine Nature.

Jesus benign a human was tempted by Satan, yet He did not submit. Jesus had acquire by His own free will God's Divine Nature, Jesus had by birth the Holy Spirit, He and only He had the full measure of God's Divine Nature from human birth, the Holy Spirit. The human mind is not born with Satan's nature, neither is it born with the Divine Nature, we chose to acquire them. God did put His Nature in are hearts, but we must submit to His nature, we have free will to do so. There is no excuse whatsoever for not knowing God.

{Romans 1:17-20 NLT}-[17] This Good News tells us how God makes us right in his sight. This is accomplished from start to finish by faith. As the Scriptures say, "It is through faith that a righteous person has life." [18] But God shows his anger from heaven against all sinful, wicked people who suppress the truth by their wickedness. [19] They know the truth about God because he has made it obvious to them. [20] For ever since the world was created, people have seen the earth and sky. Through everything God made, they can clearly see his invisible qualities—his eternal power and divine nature. So they have no excuse for not knowing God.

As soon as an infant or little child begins to exercise there brain in the thinking process, guest what, Satan's is there to broadcast his nature into the human spirit, but God's Divine Nature is all ready in place. Since the normal child minds begins receiving these impulses to accept Satan's nature very early in childhood, unless counteracted by parental teaching and attitudes of God's Divine Nature, they will automatically begin accepting these evil nature attitudes. They become habitual-by habit and than are acquire and exhibit them in there life.

Man cannot change his human nature, but God can and will. This is precisely what Jesus Christ kingdom is all about; God will use the millennial kingdom to bring about change to human nature. Now you can begin to understand what Jesus Christ kingdom is all about. Look at how our High Priest Jesus, changes our human nature when we call on him for salvation in present day. God does not change our free prerogative; we must come to repentance and faith in Jesus Christ by our own free will. Those are the conditions that God requires of us that we chose by our own free will. In addition, when we yield to those conditions then God starts the changing process. Repentance and faith are the two conditions to change our human spirit and nature.

God does not abolish human nature, not as long as we are in human flesh. However, He does upon real repentance and faith; give us His precious gift of the Holy Spirit, His Divine Nature. This enters into the mind and spirit of those who are saved. Yet it does not drive out or eliminate human nature, this is why Satan is still broadcasting to the saved, to see if they will listen. This is the battle over souls. However, if one has really repented, and fully believes the truth, they will want to lead by the Holy Spirit. And all who are led by the Holy Spirit are children of God

If one makes the decision to be led by the Holy Spirit, in him is also the power of God's Divine Nature, and that will enable him to resist his human nature, and follow God's Divine Nature. And as we resist the power of our human nature, we have obedience to God's ways and we grow in our spirit. Until the time of Jesus Christ return, our human nature will be gone, only God's Divine nature will remain. Let us follow the Holy Spirit in every part of our lives. Then we will not be doing what our sinful nature craves.

It is important to know that the wonderful Utopia of Jesus Christ kingdom will not be achieved all at once. Remember God is going to change human nature and He is going to use the millennial kingdom to bring about this change. Every major step of God's coming kingdom is laid out before our eyes in scriptures (biblical prophecy). Jesus Christ who walked over the hills and valleys of the Holy Land Jerusalem more than 2,000 years ago is coming again. He said that He would come again. After He was crucified, God raised Him from the dead, after three days and three nights. Jesus ascended to the Throne of God, now he is exalted to the place of highest honor in heaven, at God's right hand.

All the things, which God had foretold through prophecy by His prophets, that Jesus Christ would suffer, have been fulfilled. What was done to Jesus was done in ignorance. God had put this into there minds, God stirred up there spirits so prophecy would be fulfilled. God was fulfilling what all the prophets had foretold about the Messiah,—that he must suffer these things. Again, He is in heaven until the time of restitution of all things. In this, case the restoring of God's government on earth, and the restoring of world peace, Jesus Christ kingdom. It is time to repent of your sins and turn to God, so that your sins may be wiped away. God is going to restore us to the time of the Garden of Eden so we can live in His presence. It will literally be haven on earth as Jesus comes to live on earth.

Jesus Christ will return, this time He is coming as King of kings and Lord of lords. He will establish a world government and rule all nations, with a rod of iron. Thing of it. The King of kings, the glorified Christ-coming in all splendors with supernatural power and glory of God the Father. He is coming to save mankind, coming to usher in peace. But will He be welcomed by all nations of the earth.

Will humanity shout with joy, and welcome Him in all His glory? They will not! They will believe the false ministers of Satan the devil. The people, who are left on the earth after the rapture, will be deceived. The nations will be angry at His coming. The military forces will actually attempt to fight. The nations will be engaged in the climatic battle of the coming 3rd. World war, the battlefront will be Jerusalem, and then Jesus Christ will return. He will fight against those nations, and they fight against Him. Jesus will totally defeat them. This is the war we call Armageddon. Evil spirits gathered all the rulers and their armies to a place with the Hebrew name Armageddon.

Now Satan does mimic God's ways, Satan is going to try set up a kingdom just like God's. Very soon, a new leader will emerge on the scene, a man with great charisma. It could be after a devastating war in the Middle East, where Israel will come out on top.

This leader will have a plan to restore peace. Through this plain, he will quickly rise to power and captivate and control the world. It will be easy and very quick for him, because all believers in Jesus Christ will have recently disappeared from earth in the rapture. He will have no trouble persuading most of the remaining people of earth, to believe in him as peace leader.

This leader will astound and amaze them with feats of supernatural doings, of diplomacy, conquest and much more. This is Satan at work trying to set up a one world Government. The Antichrist will proclaim to be ruler over the entire earth. He will set up a one-world government empire In Babylon. But this is a false government, Satan is trying to copy God's Kingdom, but Satan wants us to worship Him and not God.

He will oppose and will exalt himself over everything that is called God or is worshiped, proclaiming himself to be God. Man cannot set up a world government, and so it will be for Satan. The end of his reign is the world war we call Armageddon, this is where Babylon will be destroyed. Then the second coming of Jesus Christ will be fulfilled. Yes, Satan's government will lead man to a world war, not all the nations of the world will submit to Satan's claim of ruler of the world, and they will not submit to Him as God.

The fall of Satan was when God Cast him out of heaven so fast his ejection resembled a lightning bolt. At that time, God did not ban him from heaven. Satan has access to God's throne or I should say he has permission to go before God. He uses that access to accuse believers day and night. Satan is still able to enter the gates of paradise until that war in heaven comes and Satan will have no place in heaven anymore. The book of Job shows that Satan still has access to God, and that Satan watching everything that is going on across the earth. This ejection is not the war in heaven that we take about.

Satan was to serve God directly in his Holy Temple. In a gesture or to say he got fired from his job. He was the anointed cherub who covers. God had ordained and anointed him as the mighty angelic guardian. He had access to the holy mountain of God and walked among the stones of fire. He was blameless in all he did from the day he was created until the day evil was found in him.

The devil will be cast out at of heaven at the time of judgment, the tribulation period. He the Prince of this world the earth will be thrown down to the earth. The devil, the Prince will be cast out of heaven. The bible calls the devil Prince and he was a cherub and angelic guardian. Although the bible only identifies only one archangel, Michael, it does say that there are others princes and there may be other archangels. In Dan., 10-13 says Michael one of the chief princes implying there are others angels of this type. Michael is an archangel and a prince, so if there are others like him than they to must be an archangel and can be a prince to.

Satan, the god of this evil world and the angles that follower him are the force behind all the evil and many of the troubles we have and he is the force behind many world empires today. Satan was the anointed cherub who was covering or guarding the throne of God. In scriptures cherub are a higher order of angles, who are assigned special duties. Satan having lost his position came down to they earth. Satan has been dethrone. The de-throning came when Jesus Christ had victory over the cross, and his resurrection. God is waiting to remove Satan, because he is giving all a last change to repent. God will remove Satan when Jesus Christ comes back.

We humans are flesh and blood, Jesus became flesh and blood only as a human being could he die, and only by dying, could he break the power of the Devil. Therefore, it was necessary for Jesus to be in every respect like us. What was done to Jesus was done in ignorance. You see Satan and the demons did not know that the cross was God's chosen method for

Jesus Christ to make redemption for our sins. In this way, Satan had a role in sealing his own fate and the fate of all who do not except the truth. You see when Jesus rose from the grave the sin bondage caused by Satan was broken. The count down to Satan doom began with the resurrection of Jesus, and will end with him put in the lake of fire.

A vast majority off people have a negative view of Satan, but flew realize they are doomed with him, to share his fate, unless they turn to Jesus Christ. The blood of Jesus is the only way to break away from sin. Unlike Satan whose fate is sealed, we have the option of choosing Jesus Christ as our Lord and Savior. By repenting and receiving the blood of Jesus Christ, it is our only why out of sin. You will overcome him (devil) because of the blood of the Lamb. Before you let yourselves, be slaves of impurity and lawlessness choose to be slaves of righteousness so that you will become holy. When we are slaves of sin, we are not concerned with doing what is right. And what is the result? It is not good, when you become saved, you will be ashamed of the things you used to do, things that end in eternal doom. Now you must choose to be slaves of righteousness so that you will become holy. So when you are free from the power of sin and have become slaves of God. you do those things that lead to holiness and result in eternal life. For the wages of sin is death, but the free gift of God is eternal life through Jesus Christ are Lord and saver.

Satan at some time will be forcefully removed from heaven, during the tribulation period. The archangel Michael and others of God's angels will show Satan the door. He will no longer be welcome in heaven or God's present. You see Satan and the demons did not know that the cross was God's chosen method for Jesus to make redemption for our sins; Satan had a role in sealing his own fate. However, when Jesus rose from the grave the sin bondage of sin cause by Satan was broken and the countdown to his doom has begun.

Satan does use his access to God's throne to accuse all believers, as this scripture says, for the Accuser has been thrown down to earth—the one who accused our brothers and sisters before our God day and night. So Satan does accused believers all the time. But he does not do as he please, he is on a leach under the authority of God, the King of the universe. A good illustrated point is in the book of Job. In Job story, Satan had to ask for God's permission to tempt Job and to test him. But God had put certain limitations on Satan and what he could do to Job. At some point, the Accuser will be forcefully removed from heaven during the tribulation period, but for now he the

Devil is accusing all who believe in Jesus Christ of sin and more. The Archangel Michael and other of God's angels will show Satan the door.

He no longer will be welcome in heaven or in God's present. But terror will come on the earth and the sea. For the Devil will be removed from God's present and he will come down to the earth in great anger, and he knows that he has little time.

The ruler or prince of this world is Satan, and he knows that he has little time. The time for Satan is drawing near to be cast out. The rapture and the tribulation are near very near. The devil will be eviction from heaven in a fit of rage, woe to the inhabitants of the earth. Satan will want to cause as much death and lose of souls as he can at that time. It is very possible that the rapture Christians will witness this eviction first hand, because the banishment does not occur until the latter part of the tribulation. The believers could be in heaven at that time. Remember the rapture could occur at anytime, although it is likely to occur at or very near the beginning of the tribulation.

This prophecy in Genesis Is the first messianic in the bible. (About Jesus Christ) The saying here is that a person born of the seed of woman will suffer a wound from Satan on his heel, but He will inflict a wound on Satan head. This prophecy is symbolic, a wound on the heel is none-lethal but a head wound is a lethal strike. The person of the seed of the woman is Jesus and the lethal strike is when Satan is put into the lake of fire. The heel strike is when Jesus Christ was put to the cross. You know that the cross was God's chosen method for Jesus to make redemption for our sins. Jesus rose from the dead, so it was not the lethal strike that Satan though he made.

At the end of the tribulation, the devil will be locked in the bottomless pit for the 1000 years. The time Jesus will rule the earth. This will be the first time the devil will be subjected to punishment, but he will be released for a little while. After the devil is released from his prison, he will go out to deceive the nations that are on the earth. He will start one more rebellion against God. Then Satan will be cast into the lake of fire, where the beast and false prophet are, and they will be tormented day and night forever and every. The lethal strike.

This prophecy in Genesis 3:15 is remarkable, it was given at the dawn of mans history. As we must wait for Satan's ultimate defeat, we will have to deal with temptations from the devil and all demonic angles and spirits. We are encouraged to put on the fall armor of God. By submitting ourselves to God, we resist the devil; he will flee from us if we trust in the Lord. We are advised to avoid giving Satan an opportunity in our lives. For we are not fighting against people made of flesh and blood, but against the evil rulers and authorities of the unseen world, against those mighty powers of darkness who rule this world.

It is best not to give the Devil the opportunity to tempt you. He needs a reason to do so, he prowls around looking for an opportunity to try to get your soul. In Luke 4:13 the Devil departed from Jesus when every opportune had ended, until the next opportune time. I have learned through my experience that it is much easier to avoid giving the Devil an opportunity than it is to resist him. He is not allowed to just come after you; he must be given the chance to tempt you. Watch out for attacks from the Devil he is looking for some victim to devour.

You should use every piece of God's armor to resist the enemy in the time of evil. So that after the battle you still will be standing firm. Stand your ground putting on the sturdy belt of truth and the body armor of God's righteousness. For shoes put on the peace that comes from the good news, so that, you will be fully prepared. In every battle, you will need faith as your shield to stop the fiery arrows aimed at you by Satan. Put salvation as your helmet, and take the sword of the Spirit that is the word of God. Pray at all times and every occasion in the power of the Holy Spirit. Stay alert and be persistent in your prayers for all Christians everywhere. The bible instructs us to humble ourselves to God.

You want to resist the devil, you do not want to do battle with him or have anything to do with him, and You must leave the battle in God's hands. Michael the archangel one of the mightiest of God's angles did not dare to accuse Satan when arguing with him over the body of Moses. To resist the devil you must make a spiritual renewal of you thoughts and attitudes. Throw off your old evil nature and former way of life. You must have a new nature because you are a new person you know you were created in God's likeness. Do not bring any sorrow to God's Holy Spirit by the way you live. Get rid of bitterness, rage, anger, harsh words and slander, and all types of malicious behavior.

This is the way of Satan, instead be kind to each other, forgiving one another, just as God forgave all of us through Jesus Christ. Ask God for wisdom to resist the devil. Wisdom from heaven is pure, peace loving, gentle at all times willing to yield to others, it is mercy, and good deeds come froth and are always sincere. God's ways are wise and full of wisdom. In this why you will be able to stand against the devil and all his tricks.

If you act with malicious behavior, rage, anger or any other evil Jesus said you are obeying your real father the devil and that you love to do evil.

{John 8:42-45 NLT}-[42] Jesus told them, "If God were your Father, you would love me, because I have come to you from God. I am not here on my own, but he sent me. [43] Why can't you understand what I am saying? It's because you can't even hear me! [44] For you are the children of your father the devil, and you love to do the evil things he does. He was a murderer from the beginning. He has always hated the truth, because there is no truth in him. When he lies, it is consistent with his character; for he is a liar and the father of lies. [45] So when I tell the truth, you just naturally don't believe me!

We humans can be possessed by Satan and demons and even Christians. The fact that we are humans and remain in our bodies we will struggle with our sin nature. Sin is the way in for Satan and demons to indwelling us. However, Christians who confess there sins to God have a shield around them and they cannot get in. Remember that if we do sin and confess our sins we have an advocate who pleads our case before the Father. He himself is the sacrifice that atones for our sins…Jesus Christ, and there is no darkness in him at all. Our body's are the temple of God and we can let it be defiled, if we let sin in our lives, why then would God protect us from the presence of evil. God will destroy anyone who defiles His temple. Know this that if the Spirit of God dwells in us no evil can.

Christians who keep the faith and know the truth about Jesus Christ are protected from all evil and this evil cannot possess them. But what about Non-Christians, they to are protected to a certain extent, you see the Lord does not allow Satan or demons to violate our free will. This evil needs a reason or opportunity to do so, a right to try to take your soul through being possessed by Satan or demons or any other sin.

Sin is a doorway for evil to come into our lives. You see there must be a legal reason before evil can actually dwell in our bodies. Sin gives this legal reason, the opportunity, or doorway is sin. We sin through our own free will, and this free will does give the legal right. Now Jesus was tempted by Satan, but He had no sin, God did aloud Satan to try to tempt Him. Jesus was made weak so Satan could even try to do this; Jesus was led by the Spirit in the wilderness for forty days and had nothing to eat.

Jesus cleanses us of our filthiness or sin so we will become joint heirs with Him in the Kingdom of God.

By we must do our part to, we must use the power and authority that we now have through Jesus Christ to cleanse ourselves of our filthiness and sins. Our sin and evil are now trespassers and have no legal right to remain, unless we give legal ground to do so. Once evil is cast out for trespassing, that person must become a Christian and come to the Lord. Or that person will be worse off than before. You see the demons will come back and bring seven other spirits more evil than itself, and they all enter the person and live there. And so that person is worse off than before.

However if this person belongs to God, the unclean spirit can not return, it will be trespassing. It will have no legal right to be able to go back into its house. It is not his house but God's temple. God and evil cannot be in the same place at the same time, because God does destroy all evil. The scriptures are very plain about Satan; we are to have no dealing with him or his demons. Do not consult with mediums or those who consult with the dead. By consulting with mediums, you can open a doorway, or peripheral involvement in the occult or any other sin will give legal rights to Satan's power and could result in an inflow of demons. All throughout scriptures Satan and demons are referred to as serpents and scorpions, read what Jesus said in Luke 10:19.

Every person must be aware of the opportunity that they give evil. And the possible of doorways in there own life. And we must have an understanding of these doorways either currently or in the past. Many people are bound by evil, either from within or from without. Their minds are bound so it is hard to understand the message of Jesus Christ. Many cannot accept Jesus Christ as their savior when He is presented to them. We as Christians must free their minds, you see the Gospel of Jesus Christ is veiled or to say hidden from them who are perishing.

Remember dealings with the occult, no matter how big or lightly your involvement is a doorway, and so is palm readers, fortune teller, tea leaf reader etc. Watch out for visualization, which can open a doorway to the spirit word and then contact with demons. Yoga is often overlooked; this is link to the Hindu God Brahman. We may think we are completely operating in the Holy Spirit, but any think that takes God out of it is unholy. This is a very important to understand, do not do Yoga as a religion but only as physical exercise. Some teachers are themselves deceived and do no they are actually teaching a religion. We must always search out all the things we become involved in, and know the exact meanings of all the terms used in are endeavors.

Watch out for worlds like…powers, vibrations, energies, higher consciousness, self-realization, your guide, or counselor etc. The Bible has numerous references in scriptures to meditation, but do not blank your mind. Satan can get control of you this way. The fact is God commands us to control are minds. There is a big difference between Godly meditation and others. Meditate on God and the Scriptures. Do not set your mind free, because if you free your mind anything can get in, by attempting to clear your mind of all thoughts this opens doorways you are not in control of.

There are so many other doorways that actually put the people practicing them in harms way, into direct contact with demons. This contact may not be known by the person, so they are not willfully doing evil. We must always be on alert to the possibility of demonic influence from everywhere and everything. With these principles in mind, let us look at some doorways that we think are harmless. Some physical therapy departments use a wide variety of medical healing that has direct contact with demons. The purpose of these are for us to learn how to arouse and control are psychic abilities, and with proper control it brings strength, wisdom but not the God kind of miraculously healing.

Mind control like hypnosis, subliminal tapes and repetitive sounds, biofeedback it produces an altered consciousness that is exposed to the spirit world, martial arts a sport harmless physical exercise and discipline yes, but these arts were developed by a culture that is saturated with demon worship. Now I would like to say here that if you do any of these things and you do worship there god's, you are cursed! Nevertheless, if you do any of these things and do not know about their gods, and you do not of your own free will worship them you should be all right. But then you must be on your guard at all times for opportunity and any reason for evil to come into your life.

If you have any open doorways to evil demons in your life then you must close them with the blood of Jesus Christ. Remember that you opened those doorways of your own free will. Confess your sin, and God will forgive you and cleanse you of all unrighteousness.

The scriptures show us that idols represent demons. And that all such things used in the services of Stan are an abomination unto God, even the gold and silver on them must be destroyed. Why? Because the powerful influence from demons, will cause worship of demons. God warned the Israelite and

Moses that they would also become "a cursed thing" if they brought such objects into their home. Familiar objects are things demons cling to, and anything used in the worship of Satan is legal ground for Satan and demons. They have a right to cling to all such objects.

Without raising questions of conscience, conscience the faculty of recognizing the difference between right and wrong.{Webster's Dictionary} The following scriptures shows that if we do not know that a thing is an abomination to the lord, then it is not a sin. But if you know it is an abomination then your are to have nothing to do with it, it is a sin. But you are to thank God for everything, and then you can enjoy whatever it is you are doing, whatever you do, do all to the glory of God.

Demonic demons seem to make a very specific effort to gain a foothold in every child's life at an early age. For instance: in a particularly vivid nightmare, which they feel, was not really a dream. To many times we pass these off as merely as a childish nightmare, or a dream. Just be on alert, not all of these are nightmares or dreams, so you can stop the demonic contact in early childhood. As parents, we must protect our children with the power of Jesus Christ, so they will come to Jesus at an early age, so we can save them from many hurts and sorrows, and nightmares. And do not forget about yourself, do not pass all your dreams off as nightmares, use the blood of Christ. Pray with your children every night as you put them to bed, asking the Lord to shield and protect you and them from all evil throughout the night. Teach them that there all no monsters that Jesus cannot defeat, and to send them away with the power of Jesus Christ, be gone with the name and power of Jesus Christ.

You should take note if your child is afraid to go to sleep because of something in the closet or under the bed; they may be under attack and experiencing contact with the spirit world or some kind of evil. Teach them to rebuke whatever frightens them in the name of Jesus Christ, you should do the same. You can simply say "Jesus help me" Children can learn spiritual warfare at a very young age. Children have a very simple faith that the Lord will work in there lives, we all should have this kind of faith.

We must also bear in mind that sin not forgiving or transgression and iniquity can be passed down or inherit. There are doorways of inheritance and are often overlooked. As it is said, "sins of the father." And remember any sin not brought under the blood of Christ, is legal ground for Satan.

There are many references in the scriptures about sins of the father being passed down to the sons. When

Israel would come together in fasting and prayer, they not only confess their sins, but the sins of their fathers. The sins of our ancestors can have an effect upon our own lives and the doorways of inheritance must be closed by prayer and confess of sin in yours and your ancestors. Especially damaging is any involvement in the occult and idol or demon worship. Sins are pass down to the "children and on the grandchildren to the third and fourth generations." God will not excuse the guilty; He lays the sins of the parents upon their children and grandchildren.

God will not excuse the guilty, He lays the sins of the parents upon their children and grandchildren Righteous people will be rewarded for their own righteous behavior, and wicked people will be punished for their own wickedness. The child will not be punished for the parent's sins, and the parent will not be punished for the child's sins, but can open doorways for Satan to have legal ground to come into your life. God does not let the guilty go, he will pass the iniquity on to the next generation, but we cannot loss are souls for the iniquity of others.

For sins of the father, we must go before God and petition Him to forgive us our sins and the sins of the father. You see Satan is going before the Father to petition Him for our soul. Satan ask God for all unsaved souls, Satan is accusing all unsaved and says see so-and-so is participating in sin or that there ancestors did whatever was a sin, therefore he has a legal right to the soul and to influence are life or to send his demons into us. God being absolutely just, will grant Satan his petition if not contested. We as joint heirs with Christ have more legal right to petition God the Father then Satan does. So counter-petition Satan in the name of Jesus Christ and ask God to forgive all sins, yours, and the father. We must understand that this battle for souls is real. And that we the power and authority in Jesus Christ to save souls and win.

We must learn to test everything in are lives, against God's word. We must search the scriptures to test and see if everything in our life measures up to them. The Bible must be the final authority in are lives. Do not miss the precious gift of God's salvation simply because you have not search for the truth in the scriptures. The truth is God's greatest blessing—salvation through Jesus Christ. Through your own free will, searching for God and making a personal decision to make Jesus Christ your Lord and Savior that you can make it to heaven and be saved.

Satan works from deception, his plan down through the ages has been to deceive as many people as he can, that we do not have to fear God or serve Him. Satan has been deceiving the masses by thinking they are serving God, but they are actually serving Satan. We are clearly warned in scriptures that many people will think that they are worshiping Jesus of the bible but they are not. Jesus in scriptures, was born of a virgin, was the son of God, was born of human flesh and was sinless from birth, paid the price for are sins on the cross, arose from the dead on the third day, ascended to heaven to sit at the right of the Father, and will come again.

Any other Jesus that does not fulfill all of these things is not the Jesus of the bible. And you will be serving Satan a false God. This is why we must test all spirits.

Failure to read and heed the scriptures and your turnings points can cause terrible damage and open doorways to evil. In these days in which we are now living, the last days. The Bible does say that Satan will work through deception and within the Christian church. The scriptures tell us clearly that in the last times some will turn from the truth, the true faith about Jesus Christ, and the bible. And they will follow deceptive spirits and teachings of demons. "As the serpent deceived Eve by his craftiness, your minds will be led astray from the simplicity and purity of devotion to Christ."

We as Christians are far too gullible, we trust anybody or thing that appears to come from the unseen spiritual world or in a supernatural way, as being from the one and only true God. We have been giving warnings throughout the scriptures that Satan will work in our time through false teaching, false miracles, false words of knowledge and much more.

We assume that because they speak about the Lord, look the part, and act like servants of God, but most of them do not know the truth, that they are serving Satan. Very few people every stop and ask themselves should I test and evaluate what a pastor says, or search the scriptures for my self. We are living in perilous times. We must always check out everyone who claims to come from God, what God? Who's God? We should make everyone define for us exactly which God they are serving, if it is not the God of the bible get out. Remember if they say that Jesus came in the flesh they are serving the true God of the Bible

{1 John 4:1-6 NLT}-[1] Dear friends, do not believe everyone who claims to speak by the Spirit. You must test them to see if the spirit they have comes from God. For there are many false prophets in the world. [2] This is how we know if they have the Spirit of God: If a person claiming to be a prophet acknowledges that Jesus Christ came in a real body, that person has the Spirit of God. [3] But if someone claims to be a prophet and does not acknowledge the truth about Jesus, that person is not from God. Such a person has the spirit of the Antichrist, which you heard is coming into the world and indeed is already here. [4] But you belong to God, my dear children. You have already won a victory over those people, because the Spirit who lives in you is greater than the spirit who lives in the world. [5] Those people belong to this world, so they speak from the world's viewpoint, and the world listens to them. [6] But we belong to God, and those who know God listen to us. If they do not belong to God, they do not listen to us. That is how we know if someone has the Spirit of truth or the spirit of deception.

The scripture clearly tells us that Satan will work through false teachings and seducing spirits. We must take a look at the teachings of Christian Churches, we must understand that these seducing spirits are working in and present in all Christian Churches. Satan wants to spread error in any way he can into every Christian Church. Please check out everything that is taught in your church, I cannot emphasize it enough the need to be continually on your guard, and to continually study the scriptures be vigilantly and test everything. Study your church doctrine to see if it meets the Jesus of the bible. We must constantly be on guard and alert for doctrines and practices, which can open us up to evil influences. Remember Satan does try to mimic everything that God does and Satan and his demons do counterfeit miracles and signs of wonders.

Do you see signs and wonders? We need to be concerned about the increasingly romance going on in Christians with signs, wonders and miracles. As Jesus said, "Unless you see signs and wonders you will not believe," a very large number of Christians seek after nothing but miracles.

A very large percentage of Christians after they receive Christ, have the idea that now they will just sail through life with no troubles. Most are asking God to work miracle after miracle to satisfy there life needs. Too many look to God for relief from their problems and not God's will in their lives. They are not looking for salivation from God, but only there desire. And this can lead them into accepting miracles not of God, but from the wrong source. Look out for false servants of the Lord who say that you have not receive your miraculous healing, or what every you might have pray for, because you lack faith or they you still have sin even after you ask God to forgive your sins. Look at the story of Job, the scriptures is very clear that Job did not sin in his life, but his friends said that what had happen to Job was because of some sin in his life. His friends did not know God's will for Job, or what was going on in heaven with God and Satan over Job. Many miracles do come from God. God does His will, not as we humans want.

We must be careful to seek the Lord for confirmation about everything, and check it out against the Bible before we accept anything as coming from the Lord our God. God always gives time to check it out, but Satan and demons push to act in a hurry before you can ask God. It all goes back to the temptation in the garden of Eden, when Satan temptation Eve he said she would be as God's, and knowing good and evil. But what Satan did not tell Eve was that the god's she would be like was demons. There may be so-called gods both in heaven and on earth, and some people actually worship many gods and many lords. But we know that there is only one God, the Father, who created everything. And there is only one Lord, Jesus Christ, through whom God made everything and through whom we have been given life.

The double minded man; this is one of Satan's most frequent and successfully used attacks in the war for souls. By accepting the doubts and fears used by Satan, we become a double-minded person. You see the mind is a battlefield and Satan attacks everyone in their mind all the time.

One of the most common attacks is on a person's assurance of salvation. He will put doubts and fears in our minds. Remember Jesus was tempted like we are, but He did not sin. And remember Satan and his demons cannot read our minds. A double-minded man is unstable in all his ways. We go to church and ask God to forgiveness, but then we doubts we are saved or we are face with temptation, and now we must ask God to forgive us again and then we become double minded.

In these last days, all of population is gaining awareness of the spirit world. Very unfortunately, it is awareness of Satan's and demons spirit kingdom, rather than of God's spirit kingdom. The new age movement is growing at a very high rate, bringing all kinds of false teachings especially in the spirit world. We are becoming saturated with eastern religions and concepts that center around contact with the spirit world. We must have a good understanding of human spirit and the spirit world. In scriptures, God teaches us that we humans have three separate parts. There is a natural body, and there is a spiritual body. And there is a soul. Let me say it again the battle with Satan is over souls.

For just as there are natural bodies, there are also spiritual bodies. In other words both our natural and spirit bodies are composed of matter, the only difference being is that the matter of our humans bodies is adapted for this physical world, and the spirit bodies is adapted to the spirit world.

We humans have a physical body, and a spirit body and a soul, existing simultaneously, yet all unite to make humans. There is a natural world and a spirit world. Our natural human body's or fleshy body's keeps us out or away from the spirit world. Our spirit body works in the spirit world. The difference between a soul and spirit, when God breathed into man it resulted in a living soul. We need the spirit to communicate with God, because God Is a Holy Spirit, and He gives life. "The breath of the Almighty within them, that makes them intelligent", Or to say the breath of God's Spirit gives us a living soul that makes us Intelligent, and God's Holy Spirit gives us life, the living soul. The Spirit of God lives in our Spirit.

God is Spirit and we must worship Him in the spirit. The Holy Spirit gives birth to our spiritual life. We don't know what God wants us to pray for, but our spirit does because of our spiritual life. Our spirit prays with the Holy Spirit with words we cannot express. Only our spirit knows our thoughts, no man can, Remember the Holy Spirit knows our spirit, and this is how God knows our thoughts. In scriptures it is said that we receive God's Spirit (when we are saved) and not the spirit of the world and we know that the worlds spirit is Satan. But to receive the Holy Spirit we must repent and believe in Jesus Christ as or Lord and Saver. For people who are not spiritual can't receive the truth for they don't have the Spirit of God. For the truth, all sounds foolish to them and they can't understand it. But we who are spiritual can understand what the spirit means.

The spirit world is all around us. And the Heavens are populated with spirit beings and fallen angles principalities and authorities of the unseen world. Our struggle is not against flesh and blood like us but against the unseen world. And against evil spirits in the heavenly places, against the rulers of the darkness of this age, against spiritual of wickedness in the heavenly places. Jesus Christ is the only one who can rescue us from the domain of darkness; in him, we have redemption, the forgiveness of sins. All things were created, both in the heavens and on earth, visible and invisible, whether thrones or dominions or rulers or authorities—all things have been created through Him and for Him (Jesus Christ). Our sinful nature wants to do evil, but this is the opposite of what the spirit wants. The spirit of evil and the Spirit of God are constantly fighting for our souls.

The story of the rich man and Lazarus, and what happened in the underworld or the place of the dead. The description of the place of the dead is as having two parts. Paradise the place where the dead believed in God the righteous and hell the place of the dead in Christ, or those who did not believe in God the unrighteous with an impassable Gulf between them. At the bottom of the gulf is the bottomless pit or Abyss. Now Lazarus the poor man and the rich man both died. But the poor man went to Abraham in the paradise side and the rich man soul went to the place of the dead hell. They both were conscious and the rich man recognized Lazarus, which he could have not done if Lazarus soul had not a body or spirit that look like his physical body.

Now before the resurrection of Jesus Christ this is how it was. The soul and spirit of the righteous dead went to the saved side or the paradise side of the underworld. And the souls and spirits of the unrighteous go to the dead side of the underworld or hell. Now we must understand what Abraham said when he said "If they won't listen to Moses and the prophets, they won't listen even if someone rises from the dead." Jesus Christ was raised from the dead.

When Jesus was raised from the dead, and returned from the underworld, He brought back all the souls and spirits of the righteous side with Him, and locked it up. So now He has the keys to Death and Hades. Now some who came back with Jesus receive there heaven bodies, rose, and ascended with Jesus this is the first fruits of the resurrection from the dead. And the rest were taken up to be with the Lord there they will remain until the time comes for the resurrection of their bodies, when Jesus comes back at the rapture. All the righteous soul who have die in Jesus Christ now go to be with Jesus in Heaven, but the unrighteous go to Hades in the underworld. And will remain there until the time comes for the resurrection of there bodies at the Great White Throne Judgment.

When God formed man from the dust of the ground, He breathed the breath of life, and man became a living soul. In scriptures when you see a small s in "spirit" it is signifying a human spirit, but every time the Holy Spirit is used in scriptures, it is spelled with a capital S, "Spirit." We die in are natural body's but it is raised a spiritual body, this is much overlook; our spirits have a form or shape much like our physical body.

And when we die we will return to the earth, and the spirit will return to God who gave it. We cannot hold back our spirit from departing, and none of us can prevent the day of our death. We have a living spirit from God. Our bodies do die because of sin, but Jesus Spirits has made us right with God, for His Spirit joins our spirit to affirm we are children of God. In scriptures, Angels are clearly defined as being spirits. And some are in the service of God, and some in Satan's service. Angels in God's service are spirits sent to care for people who will inherit salvation. Satan's angles are evil spirits and want us to lose our souls.

CHAPTER 11

THE FUTURE KINGDOM OF GOD

The future kingdom of God has two parts or phases. The first phase is the thousand years, the millennial reign of Jesus Christ. Remember this is when God will change human nature. Phase 2 is the eternal state of the new havens and earth. You ask, what will be in the first part? And what will be in the 2nd part? Now we can put all this together, before the first phase, there is going to be the rapture and then the tribulation. The rapture is the escape for the church, all believers in Jesus Christ and who has the Holy Spirit. Remember all believers in Him dead or alive will rise to meet Him in the air; the tribulation is a time of testing for those who are left after the rapture.

We cannot imagine what we will be like when Jesus returns, but we do know we will be like him and we will see him as he relay is. God will give all Christians glorious resurrection bodies for eternity.

Our earthly bodies, which die, will be different when they are resurrected and never die. The new bodies will be suitable for an eternity. When Jesus returns, God will bring back with him all believers who have every lived. We will be transformed as the scriptures say. Our earthly bodies will be different when they are resurrected. Our physical bodies cannot inherit the Kingdom of God; our mortal bodies must be transformed into immortal bodies.

God has revealed a secret; not all will die but will be transformed in the twinkling of an eye. It will happen in a moment, the Christians who have died will be resurrected with transformed bodies, and then those who are living will receive there transformed bodies and never die. Remember our physical bodies cannot inherit the Kingdom of God. These dying bodies cannot inherit what will last forever. The scripture tells us everyone dies because all are related to Adam, the first man. But all who are related to Christ, will be given a new life, by Jesus the other man. But because of the rapture, the Christians who are living at that time will never die but are transformed to immortality.

As the resurrected Jesus Christ ascended to heaven in the clouds, He will return to earth in the clouds. And Jesus is going to bring all the resurrected saints of all time with Him. The resurrected is all who where rapture. These changed, converted saints now made immortal will rule the nations of mortals with Jesus Christ. Jesus will put an end to the deceitful evil, invisible rule of Satan. No longer will Satan be able to broadcast through the air into the human spirit. However, this does not mean that the acquired evil satanic attitudes will disappear all at once or immediately.

Millions have acquired this attitude, and although Satan will then be restrained from continuing to broadcast, what is now a acquired habit will not be automatically removed. God has given us control our own minds, this is why we can be blinded by Satan's evil deception. However, no longer will earth's mortal humans be deceived, for Jesus Christ kingdom is coming. In the millennium kingdom of Jesus Christ, the immortal saints ruling under Jesus and with Him will begin removing all the evil habits that we have acquired over the years of human civilization. Millions will still hold to the attitude of rebellion, but Jesus Christ coming shall begin the process of re-education the deceived and bring them to repentance. God will begin calling all mortals on earth to repentance and spiritual salvation. God is going to bound the devil Satan in the bottomless pit with a great chain. For a thousand years and He is going to shut Satan up and set a seal upon him, that he cannot deceive the nations.

The kingdom of Christ will be a holy kingdom. The word holy is to set apart for God, it has a sacred purposes. All will be holy to the Lord in the new kingdom, the subjects or the people will be holy to, but they will still have a fallen nature and still be capable of sinning. Man will still sin, but sin will judged in perfect justice at the hands of the Messiah Jesus. The prevailing atmosphere in the kingdom will be one of righteousness. The teaching ministry of the immortal saints of the Lord and the Holy Spirit will bring the subjects of the kingdom into a superior knowledge of the Lord's ways.

Our politicians are constantly working on plans to provide care for the citizens of their nation. In the Lord's government, the care will be fantastic. As a result, people will live extended life spans, just as people did before the flood. A person who dies at the age 100 will be considered to have died very prematurely. Only the cursed will die that young! Some of those who are born during the millennium will not submit to God in their hearts. Those who rebel during the millennium will be judged quickly and will die at a prematurely age. Others will conform to avoid judgment, but they will still have a rebellious heart. This is true because at the end of the millennium, when Satan is released for a little while, he will have no trouble gathering a huge army to rebel against God. You can see chapter 12 for more on this.

Just how will this new world government function! It will not be a so-called democracy or socialism or fascism. It will not be human at all or man's government over man. Man has proven his utter incapability of ruling himself. It will be a Divine Government, the government of God the Father under Jesus Christ rule. It will not be a government from the bottom up, people will have no votes, and no election campaigns no human will be given any government office. All in the government will then the Divine Spirits beings, the immortal saints. All will be appointed by Jesus Christ. There will only be two kinds of beings on earth, humans, and the immortal saints, and all human will be ruled by the resurrected saints, who will be Divine Spirit beings that have the Holy Spirit. Those Saints who are able and best fitted for office will be placed in all offices of responsibility and power.

There will be two groups of believers on earth, the believers who have survived the tribulation period. These people enter the millennium kingdom in their nature, physical bodies. They will live in houses, do work, marry, and have children, and possibly die.

They will still posses the sinful nature, therefore there will be sin during the millennium, despite the fact that the devil is not there to tempt, but sin will be swiftly dealt with. The other group made up of all believers who either died or were raptured before the tribulation. They will already have their new glorified bodies. They will not have the sinful nature of man, and will not sin. These believers in there glorified bodies may be able to go back and forth between heaven and earth during the millennial. We just do not know for sure.

There will not be any need for welfare programs. Social security, food stamps, or any other programs like this, in the Millennium. The world will flourish under God. There will be abundance and plenty for all the inhabitants of the world. In the soon-coming Government of God, every official placed in authority shall be tried and tested, trained and qualified by God. God has planned ahead for His government. Since Adam man has planed his own human governments and has develop his knowledge and educational and religions and even God's. Man has organize his own social systems, civilization. Man has cut him self off from God, but God has the prerogative of calling to service, such as He should choose, for His special purpose. First, it will be a government of God, not a human one. Humans have demonstrated over the years that man cannot run his own government; mortal man is utterly in capable of rightly government himself

God began training man for top positions of authority with Abraham. In His day He was the only man on earth who was of strong character and wholly submissive and obedient to God. There was no argument, Abraham didn't say, but why? He simply was obedient to God. I think Abraham was being trained for a high position in the government of God. We know that Jesus Christ is Head over everything under God the father. Jesus is King of kings and Lord of lords. And we know that King David of ancient Israel will be a Prince over the twelve tribes of Israel, literal descendants of the twelve tribes. We know the twelve apostles will each be a king, setting over one of those twelve tribes or nations. And we know that Abraham is the human father of all who are Christ's and heirs of salvation, with this in mind, it becomes plain that Abraham will be given a greater position of authority than David. Abraham will be over both Gentiles and Israelites, He is the Father of both.

Those who where rapture, the changed to spirit of immortally are heirs with Jesus Christ and will inherit the Kingdom of God. At Jesus Christ coming, those rapture saints will not be mortal humans but Spirit beings and wherever Jesus is, there these rapture saints of spirit beings shall be ever with Him. It does seam that these saints will begin the reeducating of humans on the earth. The truth of God will be proclaimed to all, no one will be deceive.

The earth shall be full of God's knowledge, as full as the waters cover the sea. The majority of humans will require reeducating, and will continue throughout the entire thousand years of Jesus Christ Kingdom and reign on earth. God's understanding will replace materialism; true knowledge will replace intellectual ignorance. The human natural mind will no longer be deceive of the true knowledge of God. The supposedly educated of this earth, even the great-great minds have absorbed false knowledge. The educated minds have been filled with a false knowledge and have allowed a false sense of values in their minds. The academic system is pagan and it has remained pagan. Injected into it is atheistic theory of evolution, the creation of the universe without a creator, this is the basic concept on which modern education was built.

Modern education is a mixture of the truth and fable, error and fact. We are taught from textbooks which are supposed to be true and authoritative. The student must read and study and accept and memorize these textbooks and not supposed to question, but to accept and believe what He is taught. In exams, the student is graded on the accuracy of repeating what was in that textbook. The modern education system of the world has been base on a false and erroneous foundation, with out God. What does come from God, the educated of this world may find it to be foolishness. They have been trained in a false approach to knowledge. Based on a false assumed premise or hypothesis taken for granted, and never questioned. The majority have come to view things through this false concept of evolution. There education holds their minds captive. With out God's knowledge, man is limited to knowledge of this physical world.

In the kingdom of Jesus Christ, true knowledge will replace intellectual ignorance of this physical world, not in words taught by human wisdom, but in those taught by the Spirit, combining spiritual thoughts with spiritual words. Those who are spiritual can evaluate all things, but people who aren't spiritual can't receive these truths from God's Spirit. It all sounds foolish to them and they can't understand it, for only those who are spiritual can understand what the Spirit means. Light will replace darkness and truth will replace error. The reeducating of this world will be one of the top tasks of Jesus Kingdom, mans entire thinking will require reorientation and a change of direction. One big problem may be the reeducating of the supposedly educated of this world. They are, the worlds finest and best minds, are unable to accept the truth, not all but the majority will find it very hard and more difficult to unlearn. It may better to start from scratch, and it may actually take longer for them to come to the true knowledge than the illiterate of this world.

God's world, the Bible is the way to knowledge for now. The Bible is God inspired and God-Breathed. The Bible is a message of salvation and a free gift from God. It's God source for knowledge and faith. By faith, we understand that the entire universe was formed by God. All Scripture is useful to teach us what is true and it corrects us when we are wrong and teaches us to do what is right. God's inspired Word, the Bible, is the foundation of knowledge.

But the majority of the educated have been trained to hold this true knowledge in contempt. Indeed the educating and reeducating of the world in the coming kingdom of Jesus Christ will be one of the most important task in God's Kingdom. Now how will all this be brought about? (The earth shall be full of knowledge of the Lord as the waters cover the sea) In the last days, the mountain of the Lord's house will be the highest of all—the most important place on earth. It will be raised above the other hills. People from many nations will come and say, "Come, let us go up to the mountain of the LORD. There he will teach us his ways, and we will walk in his paths. Now prophecy uses "mountain" as a symbol of major nations, and hills as a symbol as smaller nations. In other words, in the thousand year's millennium Kingdom of God, God will be in complete authority over the major nations and smaller nations. His nations of resurrected Saints will be exalted above all mortals' nations. God's temple will be established as chief among the mountains or major nations.

The law for us to be govern will come from God's Church, which is the mountain or nation of God, Zion. The word of God will come from Jerusalem, the new world capital. The early church received its teachings from the apostles, but in God's Kingdom, Jesus Himself will be there to lead His Church. Elijah, it appears will be the resurrected John Baptist, Jesus said," verily I say unto you, among them that are born of women there hath not risen a greater than John the Baptist". John or Elijah will be directly under Jesus Christ in the Church and directly under them will be the resurrected Saints of immortals. This Headquarters Church undoubtedly will be given the administration of the new world's system of education. Also, the true gospel will come from Jesus Christ, and from this Headquarters the spiritual conversion of the world, will have direct supervision from Jesus Christ.

The principal purpose for Jesus Christ returning to earth is to save the world and develop Godly character on earth. In the millennial Headquarters Church in Jerusalem, All teaching will come from Jesus; there will not be a committee of intellectual scholars to decide whether Jesus Teachings are true doctrines. All world Churches will receive the true doctrine from Jesus. Just as the present age Christian must continue to live a life of spiritual growth and development and overcoming, so will they in the Millennium Kingdom. They will not have to overcome Satan, but they shall have to overcome all evil impulses, habits within themselves. Only one Church one religion one faith, but there will be many church congregations in every city, and scattered through rural areas. This gives us an insight into how the world will be organized. This shows us how God's world Government can and will be established on the earth in the millennial Kingdom of Jesus Christ.

World leaders today are virtually unanimous in concluding that man's only hope for saving our civilization, is in the establishing of an all-powerful super world government. Yet the majorities all confess that they are unable to bring it about.

Could anything be more impossible than for the world's governments or nations to get together in a new one-world government of some form.

Each surrendering all its power and sovereignty to it? However, this is what most top nations ask us to do. This is the ultimate aim toward which we strive. The creation of an authoritative-all powerful world order. Would the U.S. or Russia or China or any other countries, relinquish all sovereignty over to a world government. If man did make a super world government, wielding all military power over all nations, what form would it be? Would not all nations insist on having all the power or for it to be their brand of government? The majority would only accept their form of world government.

That is why Jesus is coming in all power and glory, and why He will rule with a rod of iron. Man will never submit to the why of peace, prosperity, happiness, and abundant living unless he is forced into it. God began insuring the efficiency and perfection of His world Government by training top personnel in there lifetime. In several basic essentials like the right attitude, God looks at the heart, the spirit of attitude. Also, He looks for knowledge of true values. These people we are talking about where trained in handling people and in how to make wise decision, they all relied on God for help. They relied on the guidance and help of God. They walked with Him, they talked with Him, and they listened, whether it was verbally or through the Scriptures. They sought God's wisdom. They relied on Him for every need. They submitted to, and obeyed God.

Even when Almighty God, the creator and ruler of the entire universe, does supernaturally intervene to set up His world government, the nations will be angry. The nations will fight; they will say we don't want God to rule over us. Nevertheless, God has work out a purpose and planned for every move toward the accomplishment of His will. God's first promise of His kingdom, was with Abraham, He promise Abraham this whole earth as an everlasting inheritance for him and his children. God promised that through Him all nations would be blessed. At this time God began insuring the efficiency and perfection of His kingdom, by training man during there lifetime.

Consider how superior men having undergone a human lifetime of training in the ways of success and perfection, but now change these men into the resurrection immortal saints. Now consider how that immortality will multiply their abilities and powers, with the power and glory of God, perhaps a million times above what they have achieved in there humans lifetimes. That is what God can do, and that man or Satan cannot. Compare that to the scheming, compromising, selfishly forms of government of Satan or man.

Doesn't it make you shout out for joy, to see and realize what a kingdom God has planned for us? Look now at a glimpse into the Kingdom of God, no illiteracy, no poverty, no famine. A world where crime decreases rapidly to where there is none. Where people learn honesty, kindness and true happiness, a world of peace, prosperity and abundant living. God does predict vast reforms everywhere in the new world of utopian. Can you imagine it? A world solving the most crucial problems of today. One of today's greatest and awesome problems is the population explosion. Growing populations in the world is rapidly stripping away the ability of Nations to sustain them self. The greatest rise is in the underdeveloped parts of the world.

The daily pressure of people is one of the most incomprehensible problems of today. However, God has the solution, to make most of the earth cultivatable and inhabitable. Only around 10 percent of the earth surface is tillable. God is going to reduce the bare-snow Cover Mountains, change the deserts to green and fertile land. Thaw out the ice packs of the frost and tundra of limitless expanses of the Antarctica and North America and other parts of the world like them. Making the uninhabitable and forbidding parts of the earth inhabitable. God will provide the gentle rainfall in the right balance in just the right time or season. Just thing of it, multiple of millions of acres of fertile farmland will become available and waiting to be discovered.

Almighty God, who formed the hills and mountains, will re-form them and re-shape the surface of the earth. Much of the wealth lies beneath, the earth and seas. Like oil, gold, silver and many more minerals that all remain unobtainable. But God will make these obtainable, He will reclaim the acres from the seas, and in these last days, huge earthquakes all to come, which will accomplish much of God's plain to re-claim he hills and mountains. Although this is a punishment for man, God uses all for His Good. In fact, much of the last days disaster's or plagues, God is going to use to bring about His plain to re-shape the surface earth.

Today we humans realizes water shortages are becoming critical. There will be a day when water will be scarce, wasted water through the huge consumption of industry and pollution, plus the amounts used each day by every person means the ominous approach of that day, when water will be very-very critical and scarce. The mass starvation of millions in the foreseeable future and water shortages will lead to food wars. Add to these terrible years of floods, and long-term drought in many areas and nations will produce grains shortages more severe than usual. And the lack of adequate transportation and storage facilities in some nations will have damage from rats and rodents and insect.

Whether we like to admit it or not, man has been under a curse since the fall of man in the Garden of Eden. Man has been under a terrible curse. But God has provided a remedy in Jesus Christ, the blood Christ shed for us, has paid that sin debt (curse) in full. God will soon force us to take the blessing of Jesus Christ; He will impose His will on us. His merciful rule on all rebellious mankind. He will insist on goodness in our lives, and to be healthy and filled with a sense of well-being and contentment. In God's Kingdom no longer will there be any curse.

God gave us nature laws that operate in the human body. The penalties for disobeying these nature laws are sickness and disease. Sickness and disease are only part of the curse the earth is under a curse to. God also gave us laws to live by, the Ten Commandments, God gave Moses the laws of His Covenant, in the 3rd mouth of the Exodus. Where God deliver the Hebrews from bondage from Egypt. And on Mount Sinai God put the laws on tablets of stone for all of man to live by. Man has twisted God's instructions, violated his laws, and broken his everlasting covenant.

All who rely on observing the law are under a curse, so it is clear that no one can be made right with God by trying to keep the law. But Christ has rescued us from the curse pronounced by the law. When he was hung on the cross.

A horrifying solution for the population explosion is on it way, the tribulation. One more horrifying solution could be in the making for the population explosion, which comes from God but is not part of the tribulation. All over the world, right now officials are warning of the threat of vast epidemics even the bubonic plague (the Black Death) that took the lives of millions in Europe and other parts of the world during the 15th-17th centuries. Medical science seeks to find cures for all kinds of sickness, cures for the flu, common cold, heart disease, cancer, arthritis and many many more. But man is ignoring the true cause of these disease, only treating the effect. Man is continuing to break God's laws and rules. Disease and sickness will finally by conquered through the blood of Jesus Christ.

Jesus is going to remove the cause of disease. He took upon himself the curse for our wrongdoing.

He will first start with the laws of nature, by giving the right education. He will cause man to know that God did not design the human physical body so that it would get sick. Diseases and sickness occur only when nature's laws are broken. It is not natural for us to get sick, it is unnatural. God through Jesus Christ will educate man in the natural laws of good health. God will teach us what foods are good to eat, some things that grow are not designed for food, and some are poison to the human body. Jesus will educate us in the proper diet, and hygiene, the right amounts of sleep, to drink pure water, have fresh air and exercise.

All the problems of the population explosion and the bad weather, sickness and disease all the problems relating to crime from big city living, will are by solved-and in our life time. And there will be room for all. Remember only about 15 percent of the earth's surface is habitable today, and 10 percent is cultivatable. In god's Kingdom, He will make most of the inhabitable, and even change the whole weather patterns and the placement of continents. People will return to there own lands and repopulated them. God does say that the land that was desolate and ruined will become like the Garden of Eden.

One of the major barriers to cooperation and mutual understanding has been the language barrier.

When one cannot understand one another, one cannot exchange ideas or concepts or opinions. And sometimes in translating, the feeling, and sense of what has been said is lost.

You can probably sense the awkwardness of talking to someone through an interpreter. Having different languages means different culture, habits, and values and standards, and yes a completely different approach to life. Can you imagine a world of one language? Think of the unbelievable step forward it would for the nations, if all peoples everywhere spoke, and read the same language. One great handicap to free trade or to exchange ideas is the language barrier.

{1 Corinthians 14:7-11 NLT}-[7] Even lifeless instruments like the flute or the harp must play the notes clearly, or no one will recognize the melody. [8] And if the bugler doesn't sound a clear call, how will the soldiers know they are being called to battle? [9] It's the same for you. If you speak to people in words they don't understand, how will they know what you are saying? You might as well be talking into empty space. [10] There are many different languages in the world, and every language has meaning. [11] But if I don't understand a language, I will be a foreigner to someone who speaks it, and the one who speaks it will be a foreigner to me.

You see it was God that confuses our language, so that we would not understand one another's speech. In addition, it is God that will give us a pure language. God is going to restore a pure language so that all can call on the name of the Lord, and everyone will be able to worship Him together. You see at the Tower of Babel God caused the languages to be confound, to stop the spread of evils through direct communication between people. The people had one language and they work to build a city, a city of evil-minded people. Therefore, the LORD scattered them over the face of all the earth, and they ceased building the city. Everyone was separated into their lands, everyone according to his language, according to their families, into their nations.

{Genesis 11:1, 6-9 NLT}-[1] At one time all the people of the world spoke the same language and used the same words…[6] "Look!" he said. "The people are united, and they all speak the same language. After this, nothing they set out to do will be impossible for them! [7] Come, let's go down and confuse the people with different languages. Then they won't be able to understand each other." [8] In that way, the LORD scattered them all over the world, and they stopped building the city. [9] That is why the city was called Babel, because that is where the LORD confused the people with different languages. In this way he scattered them all over the world.

{Zephaniah 3:9 NLT}-[9] "Then I will purify the speech of all people, so that everyone can worship the LORD together.

Today all languages are corrupt. They are literacy filled with pagan heathen terms. All languages have peculiarities of expression grammatical oddities from which cause misunderstandings, and can make it difficult for foreigners to learn. In most cases, even native speakers have problems with there own language. Many are in need of spelling reform, Our English is a prime example, and writing very from Chinese, which uses picture, and all the multiple alphabets all make it very hard to learn a new language. What a world it will be when all speaks the same language.

The Tower of Babel was built around 2247bc, in the valley of Shinar. This was after the flood of Noah around 2348bc. The flood lasted 40 days and 40 nights, until the waters covered the earth. For 150 days Noah and the Ark was afloat. And the Ark came to rest upon the mountains of Ararat. From the location of the Ark, the descendants of Noah's sons moved around and their numbers increased and they began to spread out. Once man had settled in the Valley of Shinar or the plain of Babylonia, (this is now called southern Iraq) there they made there city and built the tower. The tower grew to the Heavens, but was never completed. God saw what they were doing and this was not what He had planned for man, so He caused them to speak many different languages, so that they could not understand one another. Now when the different individuals found that they spoke the same tongue, they formed into groups and began to separate themselves from the rest. Moreover, this is how humankind spread over the earth. The aim in building the tower was to allow man to climb to the heavens and challenge God, and to give them an identity and security.

You can see that man knew that God had planned for Him to populate the whole earth. And they said, "Come, let's build a great city for ourselves lest we be scattered abroad over the face of the whole earth." This will make us famous and keep us from being scattered all over the world." Man though He could reach the heavens with this tower, and this would make a name for himself and they would become famous. In God's Kingdom, (millennium kingdom) there will be no need to reach the heavens with a tower to see and speak with God.

Jesus Christ and God will dwell in Jerusalem. Jerusalem will be the center of the world, and it will be the financial capital of earth. Jerusalem light will shine for all to see, All nations will come to the light, and mighty kings will come to see it. The people of many nations will bring gold and frankincense and will come to worshiping the LORD. The sun will never set; there moon will not go down. For the LORD God will be there everlasting light. No longer will Jerusalem need the sun to shine by day, nor the moon to give its light by night, for the LORD God will be the everlasting light, and God will be the glory of Jerusalem. All the people there will be righteous and they will possess their land forever.

CHAPTER 12

THE TURNING POINTS OF JERUSALEM

Jerusalem is God's chosen place, for the millennial kingdom and His plain for the ages. Jerusalem will be both a holy city and the city as the center of the world. As the songs of a psalmist says! On the holy mountain stands the city founded by the LORD. He loves the city of Jerusalem more than any other city in Israel. He also says that distant nations will become citizens of Jerusalem, and everyone will enjoy the rights of citizenship there, and God will personally bless the city. For the LORD has chosen Jerusalem; it will be His home. This will be God's resting place forever," he said. "I will live here, for this is the home I desired.

The scriptures mention Jerusalem more than any other city. Nevertheless, the Bible uses other names, like Zion, Salem, and Ariel. The Bible also gives Jerusalem symbolic names, like Mount Sinai and Sodom and Egypt. The Bible uses these names in prophecy to describe it. God assured Israel of her ultimate restoration in the millennial kingdom, following the second coming of our Lord Jesus Christ. This is what the Lords says "I will return and dwell in Jerusalem." "And then the city will be called the City of Truth, and the mountain of the lord Almighty will be called the Holy Mountain."

Jerusalem was the center of Jesus Christ first coming, and is the heart of messianic prophecy, and is the place of Christ second coming. God's plans require its presence, now and the time Jesus Christ walk the earth. Jerusalem was where Jesus endured His trail and crucifixion and His resurrection and ascension into Heaven. Jesus predicted Jerusalem's destruction and that no stone would be upon another on the Temple, because of it rejection of Him, and the persecution of the church to come. Yet Jesus predictions included the future hope of Jerusalem's restoration and the temple to rebuild when it repents and receives Him as the Messiah, and "whom heaven must receive until the times of restoration of all things" At the second coming of Jesus Christ, and the millennial kingdom.

Thus, Jerusalem will experience escalating troubles until the tribulation period, which will reach the highest point when Jesus Christ deliverance and restores all things. Jesus even revealed the duration of it desolation, that the city would be "trampled underfoot by the Gentiles until the times of Gentiles be fulfilled". The highest point will be when the armies of the Antichrist will occupy the city of Jerusalem. At the climax of the battle of Armageddon, the final assault on Jerusalem.

This is the message concerning the fate of Israel and Jerusalem. The Lord will make Jerusalem like an intoxicating drink that all the nations will gather against in the last days. On that day, the LORD will defend the people of Jerusalem, and God will begin to destroy all the nations that come against Jerusalem. The city will be taken, half the population will be taken into captivity, and the rest will be left among the ruins of the city. Then the LORD will go out to fight against those nations, on that day his feet will stand on the Mount of Olives, east of Jerusalem. In addition, the Mount of Olives will split apart, making a wide valley running from east to west. Read all of Zechariah and what the scriptures have to say about the battle of Armageddon, and Jesus Christ return.

The city Jerusalem would be, "trampled underfoot by the Gentiles until the times of Gentiles be fulfilled". This phrase occurs only once in the Bible, in Luke

21:24. It was Jesus that said this, as He was speaking at length concerning the fall and destruction of Jerusalem and the times of the tribulation. Although the phrase occurs only once, the prophetic period is enormous, and it's concept is a major component of God's plain for us. It refers to the extensive period of history when the Gentiles are the dominant world powers and the people of Israel are subject to those powers. It does describe the period of time from the Babylonian capture of Jerusalem and continues through to the future Tribulation, and the entire current age.

Since 1967 and the Six Day War, Jerusalem's has been under temporary control of the Jewish people. So some say the times of the Gentiles are over, but this could not be further from the truth. Revelation 2:1-2 predicts at least another three and half years of Gentiles domination during the great tribulation time period. Any Jewish control of the city Jerusalem, before the second coming of Jesus Christ must be viewed as temporary.

The times of the Gentiles began in 605 B.C. When Nebuchadnezzar of Babylon came to Jerusalem and besieged it, His army's conquered Jerusalem and took the first captives back to Babylon, This is where Daniel's prophecies come in to play. According to

Daniel's prophecies, the times of the Gentiles will not end until the end of the Great tribulation. The Times of the Gentiles will end with the second coming of Jesus Christ and the establishment of His millennial kingdom. From that time forward, Jerusalem will never again be subjected to Gentile domination again. And some of the most significant revelation concerning the times of the Gentiles was given when Babylon was the dominant world power and Nebuchadnezzar was King, read all of Daniel.

Following the second coming of Jesus, Satan will be captured and bound with a great chain. Satan will then be bound in the bottomless pit, which will then be shut and locked. Satan will not be able to deceive the nations anymore until the thousand years are finished. Afterward he will be released for a little while. The final assault on Jerusalem occurs at the conclusion of the millennium kingdom, the thousand-year reign of Jesus Christ.

This is when Satan is released from his imprisonment, and he will begin deceiving the Nations one more time, and he will gather an army to march against Jesus and the city of Jerusalem. The Lord defends the city and destroys Satan and his army. Satan will then be thrown into the fiery lake of burning sulfur, joining the beast and the false prophet. There they will be tormented day and night forever and ever.

Also at the end of the thousand reign of Christ, the Great white Throne Judgment will occur. This is far diffident then the judgment seat of Christ. Our status in Jesus Christ will determine how we will be judge. The scriptures teaches that every member of the human race is to be judge by God. God will judge both the unbeliever and the believer. The judgment of the unbelievers will take place at the Great White Judgment. This judgment takes place after the millennial reign of Christ, and is the final judgment. The judgment of the wicked unbelievers will result in suffering. Following the rapture, the believers will stand before The Judgment Seat of Christ. The judgment of the believers will result in rewards. See Crowns and Rewards.

At the end of the millennium, Satan is released once more; he deceives many into joining him in his futile attempt to engage in battle against God. Fire comes down from heaven and devours them; Satan himself is cast into the lake of fire. Then the unsaved dead of all time appear before the Great White Throne Judgment. In addition, anyone whose name was not found recorded in the Book of Life was thrown into the lake of fire.

At the end of the great White Throne Judgment, heaven and earth and Jerusalem will disappear. And what do you think will take it place? But a new heaven, new earth, and a new Jerusalem. These new heavens and earth and new Jerusalem will be different from the ones we have now. God will make a new universe, a perfect dwelling place that will last forever. In the new heavens and earth, nothing will make us afraid. The only water is describe, as a pure river of water of life, clear as crystal, coming from the Throne of God and of Jesus Christ, the Lamb. This river flows right down the street and on either side of the river, is the tree of life No longer will there be a curse upon anything. For the throne of God and Jesus Christ, the Lamb will be there.

{Revelation 21:1-27 NLT}-[1] Then I saw a new heaven and a new earth, for the old heaven and the old earth had disappeared. And the sea was also gone. [2] And I saw the holy city, the new Jerusalem, coming down from God out of heaven like a bride beautifully dressed for her husband. [3] I heard a loud shout from the throne, saying, "Look, God's home is now among his people! He will live with them, and they will be his people. God himself will be with them. [4] He will wipe every tear from their eyes, and there will be no more death or sorrow or crying or pain. All these things are gone forever."

[5] And the one sitting on the throne said, "Look, I am making everything new!" And then he said to me, "Write this down, for what I tell you is trustworthy and true." [6] And he also said, "It is finished! I am the Alpha and the Omega—the Beginning and the End. To all who are thirsty I will give freely from the springs of the water of life. [7] All who are victorious will inherit all these blessings, and I will be their God, and they will be my children. [8] "But cowards, unbelievers, the corrupt, murderers, the immoral, those who practice witchcraft, idol worshipers, and all liars—their fate is in the fiery lake of burning sulfur. This is the second death." [9] Then one of the seven angels who held the seven bowls containing the seven last plagues came and said to me, "Come with me! I will show you the bride, the wife of the Lamb." [10] So he took me in the Spirit to a great, high mountain, and he showed me the holy city, Jerusalem, descending out of heaven from God. [11] It shone with the glory of God and sparkled like a precious stone—like jasper as clear as crystal. [12] The city wall was broad and high, with twelve gates guarded by twelve angels. And the names of the twelve tribes of Israel were written on the gates. [13] There were three gates on each side—east, north, south, and west. [14] The wall of the city had twelve foundation stones, and on them were written the names of the twelve apostles of the Lamb. [15] The angel who talked to me held in his

hand a gold measuring stick to measure the city, its gates, and its wall. [16] When he measured it, he found it was a square, as wide as it was long. In fact, its length and width and height were each 1,400 miles. [17] Then he measured the walls and found them to be 216 feet thick (according to the human standard used by the angel). [18] The wall was made of jasper, and the city was pure gold, as clear as glass. [19] The wall of the city was built on foundation stones inlaid with twelve precious stones: the first was jasper, the second sapphire, the third agate, the fourth emerald, [20] the fifth onyx, the sixth carnelian, the seventh chrysolite, the eighth beryl, the ninth topaz, the tenth chrysoprase, the eleventh jacinth, the twelfth amethyst. [21] The twelve gates were made of pearls— each gate from a single pearl! And the main street was pure gold, as clear as glass. [22] I saw no temple in the city, for the Lord God Almighty and the Lamb are its temple. [23] And the city has no need of sun or moon, for the glory of God illuminates the city, and the Lamb is its light. [24] The nations will walk in its light, and the kings of the world will enter the city in all their glory. [25] Its gates will never be closed at the end of day because there is no night there. [26] And all the nations will bring their glory and honor into the city. [27] Nothing evil will be allowed to enter, nor anyone who practices shameful idolatry and dishonesty—but only those whose names are written in the Lamb's Book of Life.

{Revelation 22:1-21 NLT}-[1] Then the angel showed me a river with the water of life, clear as crystal, flowing from the throne of God and of the Lamb. [2] It flowed down the center of the main street. On each side of the river grew a tree of life, bearing twelve crops of fruit, with a fresh crop each month. The leaves were used for medicine to heal the nations.
[3] No longer will there be a curse upon anything. For the throne of God and of the Lamb will be there, and his servants will worship him. [4] And they will see his face, and his name will be written on their foreheads. [5] And there will be no night there—no need for lamps or sun—for the Lord God will shine on them. And they will reign forever and ever. [6] Then the angel said to me, "Everything you have heard and seen is trustworthy and true. The Lord God, who inspires his prophets, has sent his angel to tell his servants what will happen soon." [7] "Look, I am coming soon! Blessed are those who obey the words of prophecy written in this book." [8] I, John, am the one who heard and saw all these things. And when I heard and saw them, I fell down to worship at the feet of the angel who showed them to me. [9] But he said, "No, don't worship me. I am a servant of God, just like you and your brothers the prophets, as well

as all who obey what is written in this book. Worship only God!" [10] Then he instructed me, "Do not seal up the prophetic words in this book, for the time is near. [11] Let the one who is doing harm continue to do harm; let the one who is vile continue to be vile; let the one who is righteous continue to live righteously; let the one who is holy continue to be holy." [12] "Look, I am coming soon, bringing my reward with me to repay all people according to their deeds. [13] I am the Alpha and the Omega, the First and the Last, the Beginning and the End." [14] Blessed are those who wash their robes. They will be permitted to enter through the gates of the city and eat the fruit from the tree of life. [15] Outside the city are the dogs— the sorcerers, the sexually immoral, the murderers, the idol worshipers, and all who love to live a lie. [16] "I, Jesus, have sent my angel to give you this message for the churches. I am both the source of David and the heir to his throne. I am the bright morning star." [17] The Spirit and the bride say, "Come." Let anyone who hears this say, "Come." Let anyone who is thirsty come. Let anyone who desires drink freely from the water of life. [18] And I solemnly declare to everyone who hears the words of prophecy written in this book: If anyone adds anything to what is written here, God will add to that person the plagues described in this book. [19] And if anyone removes any of the words from this book of prophecy, God will remove that person's share in the tree of life and in the holy city that are described in this book. [20] He who is the faithful witness to all these things says, "Yes, I am coming soon!" Amen! Come, Lord Jesus! [21] May the grace of the Lord Jesus be with God's holy people.

CHAPTER 13

BIBICAL PRINCIPLES OF PRAYERS AND WORDS

{Proverbs 15:29 NLT}-[29] The LORD is far from the wicked, but he hears the prayers of the righteous.

Prayer is basically talking with God. You are simple expressing with your heart what your needs are, and you can give thanks through prayer. You are spending time with God. God does ask us to take any concerns to him in prayer and God will act upon it according to his will. The Bible does say that if we ask anything according to his will he hears us. Prayer should be a natural part of your relationship with God. You should be very comfortable going to God with all your needs and concerns and thanks to Him. God wants you to rely on Him at all times.

The basis of our prayers lies in the hope and faith we have in the character of God. The better we know his character the more we are to trust in Him. God likes it when we trust in His integrity and character. He wants us to spend time with Him and be able to hear Him and actually listen for Him. We should try to get to know God's ways. The best way to do this is by spending time with God in prayer and reading and listening to His word. Do not ask God to something out of His character it will do you no good to do so. God does not hide His character from us; you can learn the ways of God heart.

Be patient and trust that the Lord will bring forth good in all that you do, and in any situations. Remain faithful looking for direction and learning the whys and the will of God. Sometimes God will bring instant and immediate answers to our prayers, but most of the time you will have to be persistent and consistent in your prayers. Are you willing to do your part? You probably heard God helps those that help themselves, but this cannot be found in scripture anywhere, at least I have not found it. God is willing to help us, He only ask that we look to Him for that help and pray for it.

Prayers are answered according to the will of God. This is why every prayer we pray or need are not answered in the why we would like. This can be confusing, why would God refuse or not answer anything we request? I definitely do not have all the answers, but you must remain in a relationship with the Lord even when the answer to your request appears to be utter silence or no or you will to have to wait.

This is the most difficult part or obstacle to a real relationship with the Lord God Disappointment, frustration, and confusion are a natural responses, or worse when lives continue to be shattered and our prayers seem to fall on death ear. However, those who learned to leave it in God's hands and press on through those emotions have a relationship with God will find victory in their prayers. God ways and will are not ours.

God has a higher ability to see the overall picture that we could never fully understanding, until the day of the rapture, on that day we will become like Him. We cannot see the future and we have trouble understanding the past. Until God gives us his perspective on things we should jest accept things the why there are. God does know what is best. We can hardly see beyond our nose when we are in deeper pain or when we are very emotional. The deeper the pain or physical it is the worst it is for us to see beyond our own nose. When we give everything over to the

Lord in pray and we throw ourselves at His mercy we do rely on our own understanding.

Above all else, prayer is opportunity to enjoy intimacy with God. It is about the relationship we have with Him. God longs to have a relationship with all, thru a covenant we are in that relationship with Him. He is are Father, He did make us in His image. The word of God gives us keys to know how to pray. When you see how God moves in are lives you can line up your prayers and thoughts with God ways. If you find it hard to hear God, you must ask the Lord to heal all the areas that are blockages or walls that you have put up that are hindering you from receive the word. If there are, wounds that hurt allow the Lord to heal them. In this way, you can forgive and receive forgiveness and you will receive healing from those wounds. If you have anything against anyone, forgive him that your Father in heaven may also forgive you your trespasses.

To pray effectively you must pray out of a pure heart. Do not pray out of anger or bitterness these are not effective. Your heart should be free of these things. This way you can pray without prejudice or unconfused sin, and do not have judgments toward others so God will not have a judgment against you. Know that God is always with you. He presence is there all the time, good, or bad no matter what you may think. Learning to know His presence will take time and patience. You will need to practice becoming aware of it.

Use pray as protection for you and your family. Remember sin is an open door or opportunity for Satan the enemy to attack you and come into your life. It is essential that you pray for protection for yourself and family against spiritual warfare. You will be on the front lines of that spiritual warfare when you pray for others and you will be attack by the enemy. You must ask God to show you any doors left open because of sin or sin against you, so the enemy has no weapons to use against you. The LORD your God is the one who goes with you. Be strong and courageous! Do not be afraid of the enemy, the Lord will not fail you or forsake you God does listen to your prayers and he will rescue you as he has promised. Give thanks in all things, good or bad in your life.

Give thanks in all circumstance and be thankful for God's protection, his provisions and blessing and much much more. But most of all…be thankful for the son Jesus Christ. Give thanks to the LORD and proclaim his greatness. Be thankful and think of the wonderful works he has done, the miracles, and how much more he is going to do. Search for the LORD and for his strength continually. We will have confidence in God the Father so we know that He hears us when we continually look for Him.

We all need to be like Elijah and have his kind of in faith in prayers and have the kind of relationship that he had and has with God. Elijah was human just like us but he prayed in earnest and had great faith in his prayers. We all can have this kind of relationship, we must do God's will and follow him and seek the Lord our God continually. We must have the motive for what we pray for and ask God in earnest. You aim should no be to enjoy this world or for the world to give you pleasure. Evil is causing these desires of the world. This world is the devils until Jesus Christ comes. The scriptures say we are adulterers with this world when we love it more than God; this world makes us an enemy of God if we seek pleasure from it and not God. We are to seek God first, and then God will make your life in this world as he likes, admit your dependence on Him and he will lift you up and give you honor.

Jesus told us to pray in his name, and whatever we ask the Father in his name he will give us. Because Jesus will pray to the Father for us if we use his name. He does ask the Father for us, but there will come a time when we ask the Father for our self. Remember its God's will and not ours, we must find his will for us. Pray that God will show you his will for you. Jesus understood God's plan for Him. When he prayed to the Father, he ask him to take his cup of suffering, but to do his will and not the will of Jesus. Jesus pleaded in prayer remember when Jesus pleaded for Simon so his faith would not fail him, and he pleaded in prayer for God to take away his suffering. You can make all the plains you want but it is God who directs your steps. We should be looking for direction and learning the ways of God. Jesus pleaded in pray and God sent and angel to him to strengthen him. Then Jesus prayed more fervently and was in such agony of spirit that his sweat fell to the ground like great drops of blood, but he understand it was not God's will to take his cup of suffering so Jesus said do your will and not my.

God has made everything, even the wicked. A man plans his ways, but it is God's will that directs his steps. The wicked have chose not to believe the truth, and come to Christ. The will of God for them is doom. If you will believe the truth than God's will for you is salvation and to spend eternity with him. The earnest prayers of a righteous person has great power and has wonderful results. Don't worry about anything instead pray about everything and give thanks to God. We should keep our ears open for God, and don't make rash promises in pray, and don't make mindless offerings for they are evil to the Lord. This makes you a fool and a blabbermouth, so if you do make a promise to the Lord don't delay in keeping the promise you have made.

It is far better to say nothing than to promise something that you don't follow through on. In such a case your mouth is making you sin, and don't try to say it was a mistake that could make God angry and he might wipe out all you have achieved and take away all your crowns.

There is tremendous power in our words. Be aware of the principle of words you speak. You must speak words of faith. Declare aloud, that you are blessed and proclaim the good news everywhere you go. This is the principle of good words the positive side of words. This principle of words also works in the negative side of words we speak. We eat the fruit of our words; if we speak bitter words, we should expect bitter fruit. I was taught that "sticks and stones may break my bones, but words will never hurt me." This could not be father from the truth. I have come to realize the words we speak can cause tremendous damage to our heath.

{Proverbs 15:1-2, 7 NLT}-[1] A gentle answer deflects anger, but harsh words make tempers flare. [2]

The tongue of the wise makes knowledge appealing, but the mouth of a fool belches out foolishness…[7] The lips of the wise give good advice; the heart of a fool has none to give

{Proverbs 16:23-24 NLT}-[23] From a wise mind comes wise speech; the words of the wise are persuasive. [24] Kind words are like honey—sweet to the soul and healthy for the body.

You may apologies for your words but the damage is done. Once the words leave our lips it's impossible to take them back. The words we speak never return empty, they will go to work and accomplish something. The word that goes forth from your mouth shall not return to you void, but they will accomplish something good or bad. Our words are not like God's, his words are ways right far beyond anything we could imagine. Our words do not always accomplish what we want them to.

We have the ability to speak words of life and death, the words we send out does not always produces good fruit like God's. We where created in God's image, but we do not have his ways, and we know the world was made by his words. We have better be listen very carefully, to what we are saying, not just to others but also to ourselves. A good person produces good words from a good heart, and an evil person produces evil words from an evil heart. You must give an account on judgment day of every idle word you speak. The words you say now reflect your fate then, either you will be justified by them, or you will be condemned.

Can you remember a time when someone said a negative word to you, and you just wilted inside, and felt like you just died? Or perhaps they said something beautiful to you, and you blossomed like a flower, and just lit up inside. This is the why of or words we speak. We must learn to tame our lips and speak living words. We must speak words of faith in this whey you will not come into temptation. A pray is words of faith and not just asking God for something. Pray that you will not be overcome by temptation.

The why of words works in both the positive (the light side) and in the negative (the dark side). What is very important to us is the light side, which gives life. We can stand against the dark side with the positive side of words. We are much better off to be in the light side of words, than the dark side. The scripture speak of the words that give life. The light side of words bring life and health; a deceitful tongue crushes the spirit. The deceitful tongue is the darker side of words.

Most of us do not know how important the words we speak are to us. It does not matter if we are speaking words to ourselves or to others. Words are of the up most important and powerful force from God. Remember the whole universe was created with words. We control them, we decide what we say and don't say. I believe every word Jesus spoke was of the most importance and value. We need to study Jesus words; the mouth speaks from the heart, where the heart is so are you. Our though are words, you will want to keep you though on the lighter side of words. God knows our thoughts, he searches our hearts, and he understand our intent and our thoughts. You thoughts are precious to the Lord, use you thoughts for peace and good, have faith don't let you thoughts trouble you.

Proverbs 15:4 NLT}-[4] Gentle words are a tree of life; a deceitful tongue crushes the spirit.

If we submit our thoughts to the Lord, they will never have the opportunity to become rooted in our hearts. It all starts in our mind with thoughts, and then fly off our lips. We must placed them under the authority of God, this goes for all negative and positive words, self-inflicted or towards others. We need to replace all negative thoughts and words with positive ones. You can try something like this, I command this evil thought or words to leave my mind or mouth and I replace that though with the love of God. You will have to be diligent and do it as often as it takes. You will most likely look like a fruit talking to yourself, but you can act like you have a blue tooth or something like that.

We should ask God the Father to forgive us for every polluted and negative word spoken or thought we have every had, and for every word or thought we will every have that will be negative. Sometimes we capture our words before they can do any harm, and we are thankful those words were never spoken. But what about your thoughts how can you stop them? You must have your thoughts on God, to stop hurtful thoughts from routinely flowing froth. In this why your heart will be pure and your thoughts will be positive. Not every word is from a pure heart. However, we should welcome criticism that is the God kind from love. The kind that is not meant to hurt but express good criticism.

God will teach you how to answer if you ask him. Wait before you respond to someone who does not have a pure heart. If someone does irritate you and you must respond try a soft answer, and back up your thoughts with scripture. You may not always succeed but just being aware of the negative words can help you replace them with positive ones and this why you will release God to help you to. Trying to alter your thoughts and words, you learn to filter out the negative ones. By filter your negative words you do not only help yourself but you may help others recognize that they to will need to do the same.

When you understand why others erupt out of brokenness, anger, hatred, mistrust, or a painful situation you can have compassion towards that person and not retaliate in kind. Usually that person has never dealt with someone who can have a soft answer and will give up. Your words can bring healing to others. You can improve your quality of life and that of others by making the world a better place.

{Ecclesiastes 5:6-7 NLT}-[6] Don't let your mouth make you sin. And don't defend yourself by telling the Temple messenger that the promise you made was a mistake. That would make God angry, and he might wipe out everything you have achieved. [7] Talk is cheap, like daydreams and other useless activities. Fear God instead.

CHAPTER 14

THE KEYS TO WISDOM

Wisdom what is it, and how can we get it? The following scriptures speak and teach us understanding, and there are many more like this in the Bible

{James 1:2-27 NLT}-[2] Dear brothers and sisters, when troubles come your way, consider it an opportunity for great joy. [3] For you know that when your faith is tested, your endurance has a chance to grow. [4] So let it grow, for when your endurance is fully developed, you will be perfect and complete, needing nothing. [5] If you need wisdom, ask our generous God, and he will give it to you. He will not rebuke you for asking. [6] But when you ask him, be sure that your faith is in God alone. Do not waver, for a person with divided loyalty is as unsettled as a wave of the sea that is blown and tossed by the wind. [7] Such people should not expect to receive anything from the Lord. [8] Their loyalty is divided between God and the world, and they are unstable in everything they do. [9] Believers who are poor have something to boast about, for God has honored them. [10] And those who are rich should boast that God has humbled them. They will fade away like a little flower in the field. [11] The hot sun rises and the grass withers; the little flower droops and falls, and its beauty fades away. In the same way, the rich will fade away with all of their achievements. [12] God blesses those who patiently endure testing and temptation. Afterward they will receive the crown of life that God has promised to those who love him. [13] And remember, when you are being tempted, do not say, "God is tempting me." God is never tempted to do wrong, and he never tempts anyone else. [14] Temptation comes from our own desires, which entice us and drag us away. [15] These desires give birth to sinful actions. And when sin is allowed to grow, it gives birth to death. [16] So don't be misled, my dear brothers and sisters. [17] Whatever is good and perfect comes down to us from God our Father, who created all the lights in the heavens. He never changes or casts a shifting shadow. [18] He chose to give birth to us by giving us his true word. And we, out of all creation, became his prized possession. [19] Understand this, my dear brothers and sisters: You must all be quick to listen, slow to speak, and slow to get angry. [20] Human anger does not produce the righteousness God desires. [21] So get rid of all the filth and evil in your lives, and humbly accept the word God has planted in your hearts, for it has the power to save your souls. [22] But don't just listen to God's word. You must do what it says. Otherwise, you are only fooling yourselves. [23] For if you listen to the word and don't obey, it is like glancing at your face in a mirror. [24] You see yourself, walk away, and forget what you look like.

[25] But if you look carefully into the perfect law that sets you free, and if you do what it says and don't forget what you heard, then God will bless you for doing it. [26] If you claim to be religious but don't control your tongue, you are fooling yourself, and your religion is worthless. [27] Pure and genuine religion in the sight of God the Father means caring for orphans and widows in their distress and refusing to let the world corrupt you.

{James 2:1-26 NLT}-[1] My dear brothers and sisters, how can you claim to have faith in our glorious Lord Jesus Christ if you favor some people over others? [2] For example, suppose someone comes into your meeting dressed in fancy clothes and expensive jewelry, and another comes in who is poor and dressed in dirty clothes. [3] If you give special attention and a good seat to the rich person, but you say to the poor one, "You can stand over there, or else sit on the floor"—well, [4] doesn't this discrimination show that your judgments are guided by evil motives? [5] Listen to me, dear brothers and sisters. Hasn't God chosen the poor in this world to be rich in faith? Aren't they the ones who will inherit the Kingdom he promised to those who love him? [6] But you dishonor the poor! Isn't it the rich who oppress you and drag you into court? [7] Aren't they the ones who slander Jesus Christ, whose noble name you bear? [8] Yes indeed, it is good when you obey the royal law as found in the Scriptures: "Love your neighbor as yourself." [9] But if you favor some people over others, you are committing a sin. You are guilty of breaking the law. [10] For the person who keeps all of the laws except one is as guilty as a person who has broken all of God's laws. [11] For the same God who said, "You must not commit adultery," also said, "You must not murder." So if you murder someone but do not commit adultery, you have still broken the law. [12] So whatever you say or whatever you do, remember that you will be judged by the law that sets you free. [13] There will be no mercy for those who have not shown mercy to others. But if you have been merciful, God will be merciful when he judges you. [14] What good is it, dear brothers and sisters, if you say you have faith but don't show it by your actions? Can that kind of faith save anyone? [15] Suppose you see a brother or sister who has no food or clothing, [16] and you say, "Good-bye and have a good day; stay warm and eat well"—but then you don't give that person any food or clothing. What good does that do? [17] So you see, faith by itself isn't enough. Unless it produces good deeds, it is dead and useless. [18] Now someone may argue, "Some people have faith; others have good deeds." But I say, "How can you show me your faith if you don't have good deeds? I will show you my faith by my good deeds." [19] You say you have faith, for you believe that there is one God. Good for you! Even the demons believe this, and they tremble in terror. [20] How foolish! Can't you see that faith without good deeds is useless? [21] Don't you remember that our ancestor Abraham was shown to be right with God by his actions when he offered his son Isaac on the altar? [22] You see, his faith and his actions worked together. His actions made his faith complete. [23] And so it happened just as the Scriptures say: "Abraham believed God, and God counted him as righteous because of his faith." He was even called the friend of God. [24] So you see, we are shown to be right with God by what we do, not by faith alone. [25] Rahab the prostitute is another example. She was shown to be right with God by her actions when she hid those messengers and sent them safely away by a different road. [26] Just as the body is dead without breath, so also faith is dead without good works.

Trust the power of God rather than human wisdom. God speaks with words of wisdom, but not the kind of wisdom that belongs to this world, and not the kind that appeals to the rulers of this world, who are being brought to nothing. No, the wisdom that God speak of is the secret wisdom of God, which was hidden in former times, though he made it for our benefit before the world began. But the rulers of this world have not understood it; if they had, they would never have crucified our glorious Lord. No eye has seen, no ear has heard, and no mind has imagined what God has prepared for those who love him. But we know God's wisdom if we believe the truth, we know these things because God has revealed them to us by his Spirit, no one can know God's thoughts except God's own Spirit.

We are to ask God to be merciful to us, to be our strength each and ever day and to be our salvation in times of trouble, in that day God will be your foundation, providing a rich store of wisdom and knowledge. The fear of the Lord is the key to understanding Him. The Lord is our judge, lawgiver, and our King. We must train our eyes to discern that which is of true value to our faith. The fool shall not discern the worth and cast aside great treasure, Having true knowledge you will not let the treasure escape you. God's promises are of no avail to you except as you apply and appropriate them. God will help but only to the point, you will let him. God does meet us at every part when we put action to work alongside our prayers. We must do our part and no case is to hard for God. The world is overburdened with trouble and sickness, but God will overcome it all if we give him the opportunity to do it. Do not be to hasty and stop the opportunity you gave him let him go to work in all circumstances.

Trust the power of God rather than human wisdom. God speaks with words of wisdom, but not the kind of wisdom that belongs to this world, and not the kind that appeals to the rulers of this world, who are being brought to nothing. No, the wisdom that God speak of is the secret wisdom of God, which was hidden in former times, though he made it for our benefit before the world began. But the rulers of this world have not understood it; if they had, they would never have crucified our glorious Lord. No eye has seen, no ear has heard, and no mind has imagined what God has prepared for those who love him. But we know God's wisdom if we believe the truth, we know these things because God has revealed them to us by his

Spirit, no one can know God's thoughts except God's own Spirit.

Always remember that it is the Lord your God who gives the power to become rich, and he does it to fulfill the covenant he made with our ancestors. But search for god and not riches and than God will give as his please. Beware that in your time of plenty you do not forget the LORD your God.

Know that man does not live by bread alone, but that man lives by everything that proceeds out of the mouth of the LORD. Know then in your heart that, as a man disciplines his son, the LORD your God disciplines you. Obey God by walking in his ways and by fearing him, the LORD your God disciplines you to help you.

We need many things in this world, but we must call on God and seek him first. And then when we ask God for help he hears us, but if there is any disease in your thoughts, there will be disease in the body. Now sometimes you have disease even if you have God in your life, only God knows why. You will not receive healing in the body if there is anxiety in the mind. When your mind is at rest, the body can receive healing. Worry is an actively destructive force and anxiety produces tension and tension will bring pain. Fear is very devastating to physical well-being and anger is far worst, you must have absolute confidence in God to overcome the things that belong to the devil. Yes anxiety and tension, fear, worry are all ways that the devil will use against you.

No more hidden sin, sin of the mind is the ways of the devil and is a waste of time. Ten minutes of temper can waste ½ days work, it takes away your strength. Your strength is a gift from God. What ever you sow in your mind, you will reap. Do not give your thoughts free rein. Remember words, your thoughts will never be on the right path until you show the right path. You must control your thoughts and if your thoughts are the will of God, you are on the right path.

The Lord corrects those he loves, just as a father corrects his child. Don't be discourage when God does corrects you. Don't ignore it when he disciplines you. Wisdom is like a good friend, happy is the person who finds and understand wisdom. Wisdom is more precious than gold or silver and nothing you desire can compare to it. The path to wisdom is always satisfying. It is not wise to hate correction from God, learn to love and look for God's discipline.

{Proverbs 4:20-27 NLT}-[20] My child, pay attention to what I say. Listen carefully to my words. [21] Don't lose sight of them. Let them penetrate deep into your heart, [22] for they bring life to those who find them, and healing to their whole body. [23] Guard your heart above all else, for it determines the course of your life. [24] Avoid all perverse talk; stay away from corrupt speech. [25] Look straight ahead, and fix your eyes on what lies before you. [26] Mark out a straight path for your feet; stay on the safe path. [27] Don't get sidetracked; keep your feet from following evil.

God is the great burden-bearer; you need not look to others to share your burdens with. God leads and guides from above, He does not use natural reasoning as man. All things are under God's contort and you must allow God the freedom to shape all circumstances and to lead you to the right path. God brings those who can truly help.

If difficulties do come God will use your trouble to put you on the path or to test you, hold firmly on to God's hand as you journey on your path, but always allow him to walk ahead and choose which path is right for you. Don't walk according to your natural reasoning, but obey God's promptings and be obedient to his voice.

Listen for God and pay attention and grow wise in his ways. He gives guidance in ways you cannot understand. Don't give up if things are not the why you like, and turn away from his guidance and teaching. Take his words to heart by following his instructions in this why you will develop good judgment and wisdom. Having good judgment and wisdom is one the most important things you will do and it will help you out of sin. We will stumble and fall but it is wisdom with good judgment that will get through it, the kind that God can only provide. Trust the Lord your God with all your heart; do not depend on your own understanding. Don't be impressed with your wisdom and judgment it comes from God. Honor the Lord with your wealth, for it is God who let you have it. The people who give generously to the poor. Their good deeds will never be forgotten. Do not hold anything back when you give the Lord his tithe. The point is this: he who gives sparingly will also reap sparingly, and he who gives bountifully will also reap bountifully. Each one must do as he has made up his mind, not reluctantly or under compulsion, for God loves a cheerful giver, and God is able to provide you with every blessing in abundance, so that you may always have enough of everything.

The point in the scripture below is this: he who sows sparingly will also reap sparingly, and he who sows bountifully will also reap bountifully.

{2 Corinthians 9:6-10 NLT}-[6] Remember this—a farmer who plants only a few seeds will get a small crop. But the one who plants generously will get a generous crop. [7] You must each decide in your heart how much to give. And don't give reluctantly or in response to pressure. "For God loves a person who gives cheerfully." [8] And God will generously provide all you need. Then you will always have everything you need and plenty left over to share with others. [9] As the Scriptures say, "They share freely and give generously to the poor. Their good deeds will be remembered forever." [10] For God is the one who provides seed for the farmer and then bread to eat. In the same way, he will provide and increase your resources and then produce a great harvest of generosity in you.

It is not appointed to us to know the future nor to be able to discern beforehand God's exact plains or will for us. But God does show us turning points and it should be enough that we walk with God together on our path. We should have neither doubts nor anxieties to cloud our minds about the future.

We can rest in the knowledge that God's ways are perfect and his grace is sufficient. God's will for us and help is right no matter what comes our way. Do not look to the future, look at the present to much is waiting to be done now. God knows the future and he uses what is available at the time or moment it is needed. God does send us turning points to put us on the right path. You should have awareness of your present and future needs but to occupier you mind all the time with these things is to your own disadvantage. Try to live in the here and now, we do know our future if we believe the truth about Jesus Christ. We will spend an eternity with God if we accept Jesus Christ as our Lord and saver. Those who do not accept Jesus there final dwelling place will be the lake of fire. Read these scriptures from Romans.

{Romans 7:1-25 NLT}-[1] Now, dear brothers and sisters—you who are familiar with the law—don't you know that the law applies only while a person is living? [2] For example, when a woman marries, the law binds her to her husband as long as he is alive. But if he dies, the laws of marriage no longer apply to her. [3] So while her husband is alive, she would be committing adultery if she married another man. But if her husband dies, she is free from that law and does not commit adultery when she remarries. [4] So, my dear brothers and sisters, this is the point: You died to the power of the law when you died with Christ. And now you are united with the one who was raised from the dead. As a result, we can produce a harvest of good deeds for God. [5] When we were controlled by our old nature, sinful desires were at work within us, and the law aroused these evil desires that produced a harvest of sinful deeds, resulting in death. [6] But now we have been released from the law, for we died to it and are no longer captive to its power. Now we can serve God, not in the old way of obeying the letter of the law, but in the new way of living in the Spirit. [7] Well then, am I suggesting that the law of God is sinful? Of course not! In fact, it was the law that showed me my sin. I would never have known that coveting is wrong if the law had not said, "You must not covet." [8] But sin used this command to arouse all kinds of covetous desires within me! If there were no law, sin would not have that power. [9] At one time I lived without understanding the law. But when I learned the command not to covet, for instance, the power of sin came to life, [10] and I died. So I discovered that the law's commands, which were supposed to bring life, brought spiritual death instead. [11] Sin took advantage of those commands and deceived me; it used the commands to kill me. [12] But still, the law itself is holy, and its commands are holy and right and good.

[13] But how can that be? Did the law, which is good, cause my death? Of course not! Sin used what was good to bring about my condemnation to death. So we can see how terrible sin really is. It uses God's good commands for its own evil purposes. [14] So the trouble is not with the law, for it is spiritual and

good. The trouble is with me, for I am all too human, a slave to sin. [15] I don't really understand myself, for I want to do what is right, but I don't do it. Instead, I do what I hate. [16] But if I know that what I am doing is wrong, this shows that I agree that the law is good.

[17] So I am not the one doing wrong; it is sin living in me that does it. [18] And I know that nothing good lives in me, that is, in my sinful nature. I want to do what is right, but I can't. [19] I want to do what is good, but I don't. I don't want to do what is wrong, but I do it anyway. [20] But if I do what I don't want to do, I am not really the one doing wrong; it is sin living in me that does it. [21] I have discovered this principle of life—that when I want to do what is right, I inevitably do what is wrong. [22] I love God's law with all my heart. [23] But there is another power within me that is at war with my mind. This power makes me a slave to the sin that is still within me. [24] Oh, what a miserable person I am! Who will free me from this life that is dominated by sin and death? [25] Thank God! The answer is in Jesus Christ our Lord. So you see how it is: In my mind I really want to obey God's law, but because of my sinful nature I am a slave to sin.

{Romans 8:1-39 NLT}-[1] So now there is no condemnation for those who belong to Christ Jesus.

[2] And because you belong to him, the power of the life-giving Spirit has freed you from the power of sin that leads to death. [3] The law of Moses was unable to save us because of the weakness of our sinful nature. So God did what the law could not do. He sent his own Son in a body like the bodies we sinners have. And in that body God declared an end to sin's control over us by giving his Son as a sacrifice for our sins. [4] He did this so that the just requirement of the law would be fully satisfied for us, who no longer follow our sinful nature but instead follow the Spirit. [5] Those who are dominated by the sinful nature think about sinful things, but those who are controlled by the Holy Spirit think about things that please the Spirit. [6] So letting your sinful nature control your mind leads to death. But letting the Spirit control your mind leads to life and peace. [7] For the sinful nature is always hostile to God. It never did obey God's laws, and it never will. [8] That's why those who are still under the control of their sinful nature can never please God. [9] But you are not controlled by your sinful nature. You are controlled by the Spirit if you have the Spirit of God living in you. (And remember that those who do not have the Spirit of Christ living in them do not belong to him at all.) [10] And Christ lives within you, so even though your body will die because of sin, the Spirit gives you life because you have been made right with God.

[11] The Spirit of God, who raised Jesus from the dead, lives in you. And just as God raised Christ Jesus from the dead, he will give life to your mortal bodies by this same Spirit living within you. [12] Therefore, dear brothers and sisters, you have no obligation to do what your sinful nature urges you to do. [13] For if you live by its dictates, you will die. But if through the power of the Spirit you put to death the deeds of your sinful nature, you will live. [14] For all who are led by the Spirit of God are children of God. [15] So you have not received a spirit that makes you fearful slaves. Instead, you received God's Spirit when he adopted you as his own children. Now we call him, "Abba, Father." [16] For his Spirit joins with our spirit to affirm that we are God's children.

[17] And since we are his children, we are his heirs. In fact, together with Christ we are heirs of God's glory. But if we are to share his glory, we must also share his suffering. [18] Yet what we suffer now is nothing compared to the glory he will reveal to us later. [19] For all creation is waiting eagerly for that future day when God will reveal who his children really are. [20] Against its will, all creation was subjected to God's curse. But with eager hope, [21] the creation looks forward to the day when it will join God's children in glorious freedom from death and decay. [22] For we know that all creation has been groaning as in the pains of childbirth right up to the present time.

[23] And we believers also groan, even though we have the Holy Spirit within us as a foretaste of future glory, for we long for our bodies to be released from sin and suffering. We, too, wait with eager hope for the day when God will give us our full rights as his adopted children, including the new bodies he has promised us. [24] We were given this hope when we were saved. (If we already have something, we don't need to hope for it. [25] But if we look forward to something we don't yet have, we must wait patiently and confidently.) [26] And the Holy Spirit helps us in our weakness. For example, we don't know what God wants us to pray for. But the Holy Spirit prays for us with groanings that cannot be expressed in words. [27] And the Father who knows all hearts knows what the Spirit is saying, for the Spirit pleads for us believers in harmony with God's own will. [28] And we know that God causes everything to work together for the good of those who love God and are called according to his purpose for them. [29] For God knew his people in advance, and he chose them to become like his Son, so that his Son would be the firstborn among many brothers and sisters. [30] And having chosen them, he called them to come to him. And having called them, he gave them right standing with himself. And having given them right standing, he gave them his glory. [31] What shall we say about such wonderful things as these? If God is for us, who

can ever be against us? [32] Since he did not spare even his own Son but gave him up for us all, won't he also give us everything else? [33] Who dares accuse us whom God has chosen for his own? No one—for God himself has given us right standing with himself. [34] Who then will condemn us? No one—for Christ Jesus died for us and was raised to life for us, and he is sitting in the place of honor at God's right hand, pleading for us.[35] Can anything ever separate us from Christ's love? Does it mean he no longer loves us if we have trouble or calamity, or are persecuted, or hungry, or destitute, or in danger, or threatened with death? [36] (As the Scriptures say, "For your sake we are killed every day; we are being slaughtered like sheep.") [37] No, despite all these things, overwhelming victory is ours through Christ, who loved us. [38] And I am convinced that nothing can ever separate us from God's love. Neither death nor life, neither angels nor demons, neither our fears for today nor our worries about tomorrow—not even the powers of hell can separate us from God's love. [39] No power in the sky above or in the earth below—indeed, nothing in all creation will ever be able to separate us from the love of God that is revealed in Christ Jesus our Lord.

CHAPTER 15

CROWNS AND REWARDS

{2 Corinthians 5:10 NASB}-[10] For we must all appear before the judgment seat of Christ, so that each one may be recompensed for his deeds in the body, according to what he has done, whether good or bad.

Many Christians accept God's salvation but most forget about good works. Because we are saved by grace, not of good works. Most do nothing to advance there good works done in the body. Those who do, advance there rewards in heaven. When we are caught up in the rapture to meet the Lord in the air, we will meet our loved ones and friends. We all long to meet them in the clouds, however some time after that we will be judged by Jesus in the judgment seat of Christ. Keep in mind this judgment is not for determining whether or not we are saved nor is it to judge any sins committed. This judgment is for the rewards we will receive for our faithful service according to what we have done in the body.

These rewards will be in direct proportion to the way we live our lives. Although the gift of salvation is freely given by God, we are expected once saved to serve our Lord by doing good works. Good works is anything done in the name of the lord or for God's glory. When we are saved, the Lord opens up a sort of treasure account for us in heaven. We then have the opportunity to invest in our treasure account with works done in the body. Jesus will open our account at the judgment seat of Christ to see what we have invested in. He then will test it by fire, to see how genuine it is. Don't store up treasures here on earth; store your treasures in heaven. Wherever your treasure is, there your heart and thoughts will also be.

Jesus Christ laid the foundation for us to build are treasures on. Now anyone who builds on that foundation may use the good works they have done, or bad. The works are in the from of gold, silver, and jewels, these are good works. The bad works are wood, hay, and straw. At the judgment seat of Christ, Jesus will look to see what each builder has done, either good works or bad. Everyone's work will be put the fire to see whether or not it keeps it value. If the works survives the fire, that builder receive reward.

Gold, silver, and jewels are good works and will survive the fire. The works that are comprise of wood, hay, and straw are bad works and will not survive the fire. The works that won't survive the fire are those that were not done with the right motive or spirit. God's test will reveal what sort of works the builder has done whether good or bad.

There would be no use in using fire to test wood, hay, and straw unless they looked the same as gold, silver, and jewels.

A Christian service may look like good works, but his motives may have be bad, works done because of self-hypocrisy. We all have seen the self-hypocrisy Christians who have served the Lord faithfully for years, but through a moral indiscretion will lose his or hers rewards because of sin or wrong motive. What is important is the fact that works should be done with a pure heart with the right motive and spirit.

Look at these good works and see why God calls them bad works. When Jesus does puts these to the test of fire, they do look like gold, silver, and jewels but they are made up of wood, hay, and straw, which will not go through the fire. Bad works can be good works done with evil motives, or unconfused sin and any other unrighteousness.

{Matthew 6:1-4 NLT}-[1] "Watch out! Don't do your good deeds publicly, to be admired by others, for you will lose the reward from your Father in heaven. [2] When you give to someone in need, don't do as the hypocrites do—blowing trumpets in the synagogues and streets to call attention to their acts of charity! I tell you the truth, they have received all the reward they will ever get. [3] But when you give to someone in need, don't let your left hand know what your right hand is doing. [4] Give your gifts in private, and your Father, who sees everything, will reward you.

So you see even unconfused sin is bad works. If we claim to be without sin, we are deceiving ourselves and the truth is not in us. If we confess our sins, God will forgive all unrighteousness. If we claim we have not sinned, we make God out to be a liar and his word has no place in our lives. Rewards awaits all believers at the judgment seat of Christ. Jesus will give us crowns as an award for being Christians, and they come in different categories of service and devotion, I know of four but there are probably more.

1. The crown of righteousness

{2 Timothy 4:7-8 NASB}-[7] I have fought the good fight, I have finished the course, I have kept the faith;

[8] in the future there is laid up for me the crown of righteousness, which the Lord, the righteous Judge, will award to me on that day; and not only to me, but also to all who have loved His appearing.

2. The crown of life

{James 1:12 NASB}-[12] Blessed is a man who perseveres under trial; for once he has been approved, he will receive the crown of life which the Lord has promised to those who love Him.

3. The crown of glory

{1 Peter 5:2, 4 NLT}-[2] Care for the flock that God has entrusted to you. Watch over it willingly, not grudgingly—not for what you will get out of it, but because you are eager to serve God…[4] And when the Great Shepherd appears, you will receive a crown of never-ending glory and honor.

4. The crown of rejoicing

{1 Thessalonians 2:19 NKJV}-[19] For what [is] our hope, or joy, or crown of rejoicing? [Is it] not even you in the presence of our Lord Jesus Christ at His coming?

The purpose of the judgment seat of Christ is for reward, and it is for faithful servants to be giving job assignments in the 1000 years of Jesus Christ Kingdom. You will serve Christ during that period in direct proportion to the crowns you receive. If you have been a spectator in your life and did not do good works the works done in the body, than you will be a spectator in the Kingdom of Christ. How can you expect to reign with Him a thousand years without any crowns? It is entirely up to you how you will spend or serve in those 1,000 years of Jesus Christ kingdom. It will be the crowns that you receive that will determined how you will spend that time in Christ kingdom, as a spectator or reign with Jesus Christ.

The judgment seat of Christ is for rewards, for those who has been rapture. And they will be judged some time be twine the rapture and Jesus return. Because when he comes back all the believers who where rapture come back with him and have there crowns. John saw thrones, and the people sitting on them had been given the authority to judge. The souls of those who had been beheaded for their testimony about Jesus, and the souls of those who had not worshiped the beast or his statue, nor accepted his mark on their forehead or their hands in the tribulation period. Will came to life again, and they will reigned with Christ for a thousand years also. These people will have there judgment right after Satan is put in his prison.

The judgment seat of Christ is for reward, but the Grate White Throne judgment is for sin and punishment of all unsaved souls. It comes at the end of Christ reign, when all the unsaved are collected and condemned to spend eternity in the lake of fire. During the Grate White Throne judgment, various books will be opened revealing every deed or thought and even the one's done in secret of every unbeliever. God has recording angles tabulating every deed or thought. Those who foolishly chosen not to have their sins erased by the sacrifice of Jesus Christ will get what they deserve.

All of the sinful deeds of believers are erased, because they accept God's mercy, which was made available to them in Jesus Christ. And they will receive rewards and eternal life. One more reason to accept Jesus Christ as your Lord and saver. Do it now and receive your rewards. So you will not have to go through the tribulation, or worst yet die and not live again until the thousand years are up, only to be resurrected to spend eternity in the lake of fire.

It is entirely up to you how you spend eternity. You have a choice to make, you can pick the rapture by believing the truth and be saved or by not believing and having to go through the tribulation and then the lake of fire. Any person who has trusted in Jesus Christ will never be condemned for his sins. The punishment that everyone deserves was paid for by Jesus, when he shed his blood and died on the cross. Therefore, sin will not be evaluated at the judgment seat of Christ. Those who do not have their names written in the Lamb's book of life will be cast into the lake of fire. The final dwelling place of all sinners who did not believed the truth.

__Make the right choice to day!__

ACKNOWLEDGMENTS AND MORE ABOUT THE AUTHOR

I would like to dedicate Understanding Your Cross Roads with God's Divine Viewpoint, to God the father and son Jesus Christ, and all of my loving family. It is by God's grace this book has been made possible, and can only be a miracle. Those of you who know me understand. But to dose of you who do not, let me explain, and look to see if you can see the Cross Roads of my life. First, I would like to say that my faith has been strengthened as the result of writing this book. Their is no doubt God has had a hand in all of this.

You see I did not due very well in school, and I should say I did not try very hard either. Moreover, at that time I did not know about Cross Roads or how to understand them. My spelling is very bad, so bad that my own family would make fun of me. I spell what I hear, laugh would be spelled lafe. This was the joke around my house. Now I would like to say that my family loves me, and would help me as much as they could. And they would say you can do anything you want, you just have trouble spelling.

For me my Cross Roads all started in the 5th grade, That year my class had about 5 deferent teacher, one of them had sent myself and about 9 other to a special ED teacher. However, she said that I did not belong their with some others kids, and said all we need is for someone to teach us good grammar clearly and correctly. That year the class had to stay back, I think only 5 had moved on to the 6th grade, out of a class of around 25 kids.

At the end of the school year, there was a special meting for all the kids who had to stay back. I remember the principal saying to my parents, John has trouble with spelling and with reading and his class was a hard one to teach this year, and the kids had so much trouble understanding. (Not that we had five deferent teacher that year, and they could not teach us very well). Therefore, we are going to keep most of them back, but we will leave it up to you since we did have to change so many teachers. Also he is so small for his age, it would do him well to stay back and pick up the work he did not get. My best friend had to stay back too, I would wonder why, he was a big kid and could spell and read. (I now see this as a cross road so I could re-learn what I did not).

In addition, when I was in the 7th grade, I broke my leg. Therefore, I missed most of that grade and the beginning of the 8th grade. The school system had set up for teachers to come to our house to teach me, only a strange thing had happed; only one would show up. So my parents called the social working from school, but she said that she had records to show that they where there, and not be to up set since I had pass to the 8th grade. (Was this a missed turning point)?

One more time about my school years. It was the 9th grade and a parent-teacher meting. I remember this one for three reason. The first was that I was on a gymnastics team, and we had put on a show for that meting. Second, all my teacher said that I was doing very well in there class. Third is what my English teacher told my parents, that I had trouble with spelling and reading correctly, that I had some trouble with pronounce and articulate my words. Because she believed that, I did not hear words right to be able to understand them. Moreover, to look into getting some help for me. (One more turning point).

One good think did come out of that, my teacher said she would take me over all her students and that if I was in a lock room with the president of the USA, and have a conversation with him, that she would bet I would come out on top of it. In addition, that this would be the majority consensus with all who would be in that room.

My school years where hard on me yes, but harder on my faith. My trouble with school cause me to be a backslider in my faith, my faith had become thin. I did not lose all my faith but I was confused. I had many my question then answers to my prayers. You see I knew that if I would ask God for help in school that he would get me through it. So I would pray for God to teach me how to spell, but to me that pray fell on deft ears. I even made a promise that I knew I would not be able to keep. That in return I would stop all my transgressions. (One more turning point for faith).

I remember thinking why have faith, if God does not hear me? I would ask why can't I spell? I did ask for you to help me, all you have to do is say it and it will be. Are you going to help me or not. Did I do something wrong, can you hear my prayers? I thought if you ask God for anything he would give it to you. Moreover, that you would get it immediately. I had trouble believing that God gave grace freely, and it was up to the individual free will and responsibility to receive it.

My faith as I knew it, and how my journey with faith began. It began as a Methodist. A member of a protestant Christian denomination whose theology teachings of John and Charles Wesley and others began in England in the early 18th century. The way that I understand it is base on doctrines of free grace and individual responsibility.

Now I know that God did not fail me, I can see how the school system failed me. I often wonder how may kids this does happen to. Now why do I say this, the school system and not God had failed me. You see God does answer all our prayers, sometimes the effects are not see immediately, and some time God does say no. God does know that what we ask for is not right for us or it may not be His will for us. (A turning point for me) understanding.

You can say God did not help me, but you are wrong you see I made it though school and with out reading a book, or without being able to spell will. I had a way of writing book reports with out reading the whole thing, and I would jest memorize some of the spelling words, I would get a passing grade for it. You see while I was in School, God did not say no to me. He said that I had to wait, until I did my part, so He could help me. I did not try to learn. All I wanted was for God to jest give it to me. However, you must do you part so God has the opportunity to help you. You see I did not do my part, He was waiting for me, so He could use it help me. My part was what God had required of me, to try and learn.

I knew nothing about doing my part. You see we must ask for understanding and adopt these principles and wait for God's help. Ask God and then give Him the opportunity to help you. Look for your Cross Roads and Turning Points in life and the ones that are all around us now, the end of days. The scriptures say to give God time to answer your prayers. In addition, God will use all your Cross Roads for your good. You see God uses everything good or bad for His will. God made everything, even the wicked. A man plans his ways, but it is God's will that directs his steps. Do not worry about anything, instead pray about everything, and give thanks to God, we will need to keep our eyes and ears open and be looking for turning points.

Remember its God's will and not ours, we must find His will for us, and then pray that He will show us the way, so we can do His will. You can make all the plains you want, but it is God who directs your steps. We need to learn the ways of God through the Scriptures. Jesus pleaded in pray and God sent an angle to strengthen him, and Jesus prayed more fervently and was in such agony of his spirit that sweat fell to the ground like great drops of blood, but Jesus understood it was not God's will to take His cup of suffering, so Jesus said do your will and not my.

So you ask, ok were is that miracle you talk about? You might have missed some turning points, but there were no miracles there. Nevertheless, I say yes, there were only missed ones. I am not writing anything new here, but on the other hand perhaps in a new light. In addition, I am not free of sin or holier-than-thou, but God does not remember any of my sins, this I know for sure. When Jesus Christ served as a sacrifice for our sins, He solved the sin problem for good, not only my sins but also that of anyone who ask and believes in Him. Yes, all have sin and fall short, short of Gold's glory.

The miracle is that I did not lose my faith. We all must endure many trials and go through tribulations. These trials are necessary to test are faith, to show that we can stay strong and pure. Remember if your faith remains strong after being tried by fiery trials, it will bring you much praise, glory, and honor on the day when Jesus Christ is revealed to all. Our faith is far more precious to God than mere Gold. Our reward for trusting him will be are salvation.

The miracle is this book, remember my schooling. Now some of you may not believe me when I say with absolute certainty that God had a hand in the writing of this book. I have had a lot time on my hands, so I would read the Bible and other books. In addition, I would ask God to give me understand. I like to say here that most of this book was for my understanding, but God does use everything for his will. So when I would talk to my family and friends about all the Cross Roads that I would see each and every day. I had a though to put down with pen and paper. Then I said to my wife that I was going to write down for her the turning points we were talking about so she would have them. Then it came to me, just write a book. However, how, I have trouble spelling and I do not know how to write or even begin. Then it come to me to just start, but how? An again my answer was just start.

Therefore, I would ask God about a subject, and then it was just there for me to start writing. I would read a page in the Bible only to find it was about something else to write about. Scriptures would just come to me, on subjects that I did not know even existed. I remember using the computer to look up scripture, but somehow I would look up the wrong scripture, but that was the scripture that I would need for something else. This would happen a lot to me. I know I would be looking up John 21 but some how I would be in Hebrews 13. Only by the hand of God! We do not know God ways, but he sure does it in funning ways.

My hope is that you will grow in Christ, and be equally challenged to see your turning points. I pray that God the Father and Son Jesus will speak to you heart from these pages and bring you into fellowship with him. Whether you are just beginning your Christian walk or have been a Christian a very time.

THESE SCRIPTURES HAD A HAND IN THE WRITING OF THIS BOOK.

{1 Timothy 1:12 NLT}
I thank Christ Jesus our Lord, who has given me strength to do his work. He considered me trustworthy and appointed me to serve him,

{1 Timothy 1:15 NLT}
This is a trustworthy saying, and everyone should accept it: "Christ Jesus came into the world to save sinners"—and I am the worst of them all.

{1 Timothy 1:16 NLT}
But God had mercy on me so that Christ Jesus could use me as a prime example of his great patience with even the worst sinners. Then others will realize that they, too, can believe in him and receive eternal life.

{1 Timothy 1:17 NLT}
All honor and glory to God forever and ever! He is the eternal King, the unseen one who never dies; he alone is God. Amen.

John R. Spiker Ordained Minister
By the Universal Life Church Monastery *9-24-2011*
Non-denominational Christian
His Way fellowship Christian Church Minister

HIS WAY FELLOWSHIP CHRISTIAN CHURCH BELIEFS ARE:

{1 Corinthians 1:10 NLT}-[10] I appeal to you, dear brothers and sisters, by the authority of our Lord Jesus Christ, to live in harmony with each other. Let there be no divisions in the church. Rather, be of one mind, united in thought and purpose.

{John 15:16 NLT}

You didn't choose me. I chose you. I appointed you to go and produce lasting fruit, so that the Father will give you whatever you ask for, using my name.

The Universal Life Church Monastery believes in the rights of all people from all faiths. To practice their beliefs regardless of what those beliefs are. And proclaim *"We are children of the same universe"* and I like to ad of the same God. Also, each Minster or Clergy member has the right to choose their own spiritual path.

I believe it is up to each individual to determine what is right as long as it does not infringe upon the rights of others or their laws. All people should be accepted regardless of their faith. Our will is supreme in our life. Even the Holy Spirit of God does not violate it. God give us all free will. We are ruling over our lives and affairs, over things that concern us personally and the things that have an impact and influence upon others. In addition, each person has the right to choose his or her own spiritual path. However, all paths must lead to Jesus Christ and God the Father.

25 FUNDAMENTAL BELIEFS OF HIS WAY FELLOWSHIP CHRISTIAN CHURCH

1. That all Christians are ordained by the Holy Spirit to spread the gospel of Jesus Christ.

2. That the Holy Bible is God's word and that all scriptures is God-Breathed.
3. The Holy Bible is the supreme authority in all matters of faith and conduct.
4. That you must follow your convictions.
5. If you do anything you think is not right, you are sinning. And must ask God to forgive you.
6. In one God, and existent in three persons—Father, Son, Holy Spirit.
7. That God is mercifully in the affairs of men, that He hears and answers our prayers.
8. That by the way of Jesus Christ saves us from sin and death.
9. Jesus Christ is divine and eternal and the only begotten son of God.
10. Jesus was conceived of the Holy Spirit, born of the Virgin Mary.
11. That Jesus lived a sinless life.
12. Jesus was resurrection from the dead, He ascension to the right hand of the Father.
13. Jesus will return in power and glory and will judge all according to their deeds.
14. All praise goes to God, the Father and the son our Lord Jesus Christ.
15. We have a priceless inheritance kept in heaven for us, in the from of Jesus Christ.
16. We will have to endure many trials.

17. Salvation is not a reward for the good things we have done
18. God saved us by His grace; it is a free gift from God.
19. God's grace rules instead of the Law, giving us right standing with God. Resulting in eternal life through Jesus Christ our Lord. The Law was our guardian until Christ came. (Ten Commandments)
20. In living a life of goodness and peace and joy in the Holy Spirit.
21. That we are Baptist with water and oil, which now saves us and it, is effective because of the resurrection of Jesus Christ.
22. That Jesus Baptist us with the Holy Spirit.
23. In the Repenting of sins and believing in Jesus we will be receiving eternal life.
24. There is one Lord, one faith, one baptism, and one God and Father, who is over all and in all and living through all.(Christianity)
25. All have been united with Christ in baptism.

***

It is all you need:
It is God that will supply whatever it is that you need.
It is God as the sun to the flower.
It is God as the oceans to the fish.

It is God as the sky to the birds.
It is comfort. It is courage.
It is healing. It is guidance.
It is forgiveness. It is God's love and grace
It is all you need.

By, Rev. John R. Spiker

God's love is here to stay:

God's love is here to stay; God's love is the way, Seek God's love
Each and every day and you will find your way.
God's love is a warm summer day.
God's love is a gentle rain.
God's love is as fresh as new falling snow.
God's love is for you.
God's love comes in summer, spring, winter, and fall.
God's love is free to all.
You do not have to look for God's love, or search high or low.
It is here and there and everywhere. Ask and you will receive. Look and you will find.
Open your hearts now for it is never to late for God's love.

By,
Rev. John R. Spiker
September 2011

Would you like to see your manuscript become a book?

If you are interested in becoming a PublishAmerica author, please submit your manuscript for possible publication to us at:

acquisitions@publishamerica.com

You may also mail in your manuscript to:

**PublishAmerica
PO Box 151
Frederick, MD 21705**

We also offer free graphics for Children's Picture Books!

www.publishamerica.com

PublishAmerica

CPSIA information can be obtained at www.ICGtesting.com
Printed in the USA
BVOW032204100612

292177BV00001B/38/P

9 781462 678730